FINAL TIE
THE INTERWAR FA CUP FINALS

The FA Cup. This is the third trophy, the first having been stolen and the second presented to Lord Kinnaird. This current trophy, first presented in 1911, was made in Bradford. The first winners of it were Bradford City.

FINAL TIE

THE INTERWAR FA CUP FINALS

Compiled by
Norman Shiel

TEMPUS

First published 1999
Copyright © Norman Shiel, 1999

Tempus Publishing Limited
The Mill, Brimscombe Port,
Stroud, Gloucestershire, GL5 2QG

ISBN 0 7524 1669 3

Typesetting and origination by
Tempus Publishing Limited
Printed in Great Britain by
Midway Clark Printing, Wiltshire

For George and Harry.

Present and forthcoming football titles from Tempus Publishing:

Anfield Voices
Bristol Rovers FC
Bury FC
Burnley FC
Cardiff City FC 1899-1947
Cardiff City FC 1947-1971
Charlton Athletic FC
Crewe Alexandra FC
Crystal Palace FC
Exeter City FC
Gillingham FC
Hull City FC
Leeds United FC
Merthyr Tydfil FC
Newport County
Oxford United FC
Plymouth Argyle FC
Reading FC
Roker Park Voices
Sheffield United FC
Sunderland FC
Swansea Town FC 1912-1964
Torquay United FC
Tranmere Rovers FC
Watford FC

For a full list of our sports titles please call 01453 883300.

Contents

Acknowledgements   6

Introduction   7

1.   Before Wembley   9

2.   The Empire Stadium   27

3.   The Welsh Challenge   47

4.   Transition   67

5.   The Drift to War   95

The Finals
1920-1939

1920	Aston Villa 1 Huddersfield Town 0
1921	Tottenham Hotspur 1 Wolverhampton Wanderers 0
1922	Huddersfield Town 1 Preston North End 0
1923	Bolton Wanderers 2 West Ham United 0
1924	Newcastle United 2 Aston Villa 0
1925	Sheffield United 1 Cardiff City 0
1926	Bolton Wanderers 1 Manchester City 0
1927	Cardiff City 1 Arsenal 0
1928	Blackburn Rovers 3 Huddersfield Town 1
1929	Bolton Wanderers 2 Portsmouth 0
1930	Arsenal 2 Huddersfield Town 0
1931	West Bromwich Albion 2 Birmingham City 1
1932	Newcastle United 2 Arsenal 1
1933	Everton 3 Manchester City 0
1934	Manchester City 2 Portsmouth 1
1935	Sheffield Wednesday 4 West Bromwich Albion 2
1936	Arsenal 1 Sheffield United 0
1937	Sunderland 3 Preston North End 1
1938	Preston North End 1 Huddersfield Town 0
1939	Portsmouth 4 Wolverhampton Wanderers 1

Acknowledgements

Most of the items and illustrations are my own but I am indebted to the following for their help over the others: The Football Association, Ceri Stennet, Dick Pym jnr., Doris Blackmore, Richard Fryer, my son George for typing, and most especially to my wife Bridget.

Introduction

The Football Association Challenge Cup Competition is the oldest and the greatest of all football competitions. From humble beginnings, involving just a few teams, most of which mean little or nothing to modern spectators, it progressed rapidly and by the last year of Queen Victoria's reign could attract the first attendance of over 100,000. That was also the last year in which a team from outside the Football League would win the trophy. At this time some teams, such as Chelsea (whose ground was to be a venue for finals), or Huddersfield Town (who figured in five inter-war finals) had not even come into being.

The twenty finals played between the two wars embrace much more than just the football. They are a reflection of economic and social change over two decades, as a nation which had struggled from the costly victory of the first war sank into another war a generation later. This period begins in an atmosphere redolent with victory, as depicted on the programme covers, and moves to the celebration of the greatest Empire the world has ever known; yet ends with another call to arms. It is also during this time that radio becomes almost universal and the infant medium of television just begins to flex its muscles. For most people who could not actually get to the Finals, however, it was the cinema that gave them brief, flickering, severely edited (and initially silent) highlights of the game. The media may have virtually taken over major matches now, but even between the wars the impact was noticeable. Newspapers and newsreels vied for custom and promoted themselves at the matches and in the programmes: there was even a toast to the press at a post-match banquet.

It is difficult to keep a balanced perspective on the enormous difference in prices between the interwar years and the present day. A whole generation has grown up never knowing shillings and pence, let alone their purchasing power, and now we appear to be on the threshold of another major change with all its implications. It is all a far cry from the 1930s when FA treasurer Huband could assure continental referees that the value of the British pound never changed – so neither therefore, should their expenses claims. The programmes, both in terms of cover price and, especially, the prices of items advertised in them, afford a microcosm of the economic situation between the wars. Tobacco products, from which sport generally now seeks to disentangle itself, were widely promoted, not least by players themselves; the prolific by-product, the cigarette card, is an important body of evidence for the football of the day.

The players were, indeed, to some degree stars, yet in another way they were simply hired hands, tied down by constraints which, despite the best efforts of the Players' Union, remained largely in place until the 1960s. However much the gate receipts were, the players' pay and bonus were rigidly controlled and even their gifts for Cup Final triumphs were modest by any standards. Even so, the players at the more successful clubs were significantly better off than most of those who went to watch them. Football was cheap – it was in no position to be anything else – and it was watched in conditions which many of us will recall with affection but which are now no more.

Individual clubs rise and fall over time. Between the wars Manchester United slid in and out of the Division One but never reached a Cup Final. Huddersfield Town reached five and were the country's leading team in the 1920s. Several other teams, such as Wolves, Preston, Sheffield United and Cardiff, have known life in all the divisions in recent years. A few clubs, such as Arsenal, have managed to stay at or near the top throughout. Individuals also stand out as well as teams. What a wonderful career record for Clem Stephenson, who played in his first Cup Final in 1913 and was involved in five more, his last in 1938.

In this book it has not been possible to do much more than give a broad-based flavour of a great sporting event. It is a mixture of the familiar and the new and, hopefully, there will be something for everyone who has experienced the unique magic of the FA Cup Final and who is interested in gaining some familiarity with what it was like in the years between the wars.

Norman Shiel.

The Medals. Initially only the winners received medals, in gold and of simple design. The designs shown here were introduced towards the end of the nineteenth century and remained in use with only minor changes thereafter.

One
Before Wembley

Rapidly growing crowds meant that the Cup Final had outgrown its original home at the Oval by 1892. After two years in the North a new home was found, back in the capital at the Crystal Palace. Here, truly vast crowds could be, and were, accommodated: how much many of them could actually see is another matter. This aerial view shows the ground long after it had ceased to be used for big matches.

A photograph showing a close-up of the crowds building up at the old Crystal Palace ground. The crude nature of the terracing and the complete absence of crash barriers are evident. The sports ground was, of course, only one part of the very much larger Crystal Palace complex.

The grandstands at the Crystal Palace ground were quite good by the standards of the day but once crowds elsewhere rose above comfort and safety levels of even a basic sort, then few indeed outside those stands saw much of the game. There is no record of crowd trouble at the twenty finals played here, even though crowds exceeded 100,000 on three occasions.

As it was initially believed that the Great War would be a short one, the FA Cup Competition carried on, with the 1915 Final being played at Old Trafford. Once it was clear that the conflict would drag on, the competition ceased and did not resume until 1919. By then, after years of use as a war service depot, the Crystal Palace was no longer suitable to stage a major event, although it continued in use for football generally for some decades. Chelsea's ground at Stamford Bridge was chosen for the first post-war Final, although the home club's success in reaching the semi-final stage almost caused embarrassment. The programme cover (right) is superbly imposing and of a classical style, redolent with symbols of victory. At sixpence it was expensive but, with twenty pages, far more substantial than the large single sheets sold for a penny at the Crystal Palace. The centre spread (below) shows the teams – an interesting contrast between established giants Villa (double winners in 1897, winners again in 1905 and with four players left from the victory in 1913) and new boys Huddersfield, formed as recently as 1908 and almost bankrupt just after the war.

The
OFFICIAL
Souvenir
PROGRAMME

ASTON VILLA   HUDDERSFIELD TOWN

Aston Villa
Blackburn Rovers
Blackpool
Bury
Barnsley
Bradford City
Clapham Rovers
Everton
Manchester United
Manchester City
Notts County
Notts Forest
Newcastle Utd
Old Carthusians
Old Etonians
Oxford Univ

Preston N.E.
Royal Engineers
Sheffield Wed
Sheffield Utd
Tottenham Hr
Wanderers
West Bromwich
Albion
Wolverhampton
Wanderers

1919-20

of the
FINAL TIE
FOOTBALL ASSOCIATION
CHALLENGE CUP
COMPETITION

STAMFORD BRIDGE S.W.

APRIL 24 1920

BERNHARD HUGH

PRICE SIXPENCE

ASTON VILLA v. HUDDERSFIELD TOWN.

Saturday, April 24th, 1920. ——— Kick-off 3 p.m.

ASTON VILLA (Claret and Light Blue).

1
HARDY
Goal.

2
SMART
Right Back.

3
WESTON
Left Back.

4
DUCAT
Right Half.

5
BARSON
Centre Half.

6
MOSS
Left Half.

7
WALLACE
Outside Right.

8
KIRTON
Inside Right.

9
WALKER
Centre.

10
STEPHENSON
Inside Left.

11
DORRELL
Outside Left.

12
ISLIP
Outside Left.

13
SWANN
Inside Left.

14
TAYLOR
Centre.

15
MANN
Inside Right.

16
RICHARDSON
Outside Right.

17
WATSON
Left Half.

18
WILSON
Centre Half.

19
SLADE
Right Half.

20
BULLOCK
Left Back.

21
WOOD
Right Back.

22
MUTCH
Goal.

HUDDERSFIELD TOWN (Blue and White).

Referee—Mr. J. T. HOWCROFT (Bolton). Linesmen—Mr. H. A. AYLING (Southwick, Sussex) and Mr. A. SCHOLEY (Sheffield).

Prince Henry, the King's third son, was presented to the teams before the first postwar Final. The then Prince of Wales had agreed to become patron of the FA in 1892 and confirmed the royal patronage upon his accession as Edward VII. It was not until 1914 that the reigning monarch (by then George V) attended a Final in person. Finals have, however, ever since been honoured by the presence of a member of the Royal Family, albeit by no means necessarily the monarch.

The two captains, Bullock of Huddersfield and Ducat of Aston Villa (an international at both football and cricket), meet for the toss with referee J.T. Howcroft. Howcroft was widely regarded as the senior referee of his day: firm, fair and respected at home and abroad. This was a 'well deserved and perhaps rather long-deferred recognition' for his contribution, as the programme puts it. Howcroft often officiated wearing not only a jacket but also a cap. By this time things had moved on from the days when refereeing Finals was the monopoly of a few senior figures such as Marindin, who had controlled no fewer than eight.

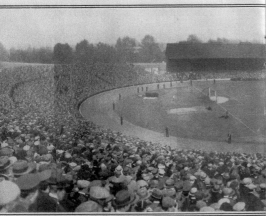

The Fight for the Cup—General View of the Stamford Bridge Ground, where Aston Villa and Huddersfield Met on Saturday Last

This panoramic view of the 1920 Final from the *Sphere Magazine* (by no means exclusively devoted to football despite its name) captures the flavour of the big occasion at Stamford Bridge. No longer the wide open spaces and picnic atmosphere of the Crystal Palace, this was a purpose-built sports ground which did not greatly change until quite recently and the capacity of which was in no way taxed by the crowd of just over 50,000. Precious few spectators got either a seat or protection from the elements – factors which mattered rather more the following year.

The Aston Villa goalkeeper was the peerless Sam Hardy, regarded by some as England's best ever custodian. The Scot Alex Mutch was in goal for Huddersfield. He had moved to Town from Aberdeen and made his debut in Huddersfield's first ever League match in 1910. In this Final, despite a string of excellent saves, he was to concede the only goal of the game in extra time, but he would soon be back as a winner. Later, he was to become a devoted and popular servant of Newcastle, as player and then physiotherapist.

Andy Ducat receives the trophy from Prince Henry after a 1-0 victory in extra time. Previously, drawn games had gone to a replay after the ninety minutes were up. The goal itself, scored in the 100th minute, is credited to Kirton, although there is some uncertainty as he went up for a hanging corner with Town defender Wilson. Huddersfield had never really looked like scoring and so lost their first Cup Final. However, later that same year came a momentous boost to their fortunes with the appointment of a new manager, Herbert Chapman.

The victorious Aston Villa team of 1920 with the FA Cup. From left to right, back row: G.B. Ramsay (secretary), Smart, T. Bate (director), F.W. Rinder (chairman), Hardy, F. Miles (trainer), Moss, H. Spencer (director). Front row: J. Devey (director), Kirton, Ducat, Walker, Stephenson, J. Jones (director). On the ground: Wallace, Barson, Weston, Dorrell. Weston, Wallace, Hardy and Stephenson collected their second winners' medals and Villa were now the most successful FA Cup side with six victories in seven Finals. They would play in another Final soon but not be victorious again until 1957.

The cover of the 1921 Cup Final programme is a much less complicated example of Bernard Hughs' elegant artwork – still with victory very much the main motif. The cover price remained sixpence, although this year's issue contained four fewer pages for the money. Note the ball on which Victory is standing is the old fashioned design, which had long since been superseded. Such an obsolete ball can be found in the artwork of most programmes for Cup Finals of this decade and in fact almost up until the Second World War.

The whole of page 10 of the programme in 1921 was devoted to the match officials (including a portrait of the referee with an up-to-date ball!). Job Davies was from Rainhill and is described rather quaintly as, 'prompt and firm in his decisions – a thoroughly workmanlike referee'. Charles Austin, of Kidderminster, was chairman of the Worcestershire FA, a combination of duties sadly no longer allowed. Claud Newman, the other linesman, was from Reading.

The Wolverhampton Wanderers team for the 1921 FA Cup Final. The Wolves had last played in a Final in 1908 when, with the famous amateur player Revd K.R.G. Hunt in their side, they had defeated the mighty Newcastle 3-1. There were no players from that year left in the side by 1921.

The relatively rare presence of a London side in the Final ensured a large crowd, despite increased admission charges (which were deliberately introduced to keep the attendance to a manageable level). Another way of keeping the crowd within bounds was by shouting at it through a megaphone, as shown here. With well over 70,000 present, quite a number spilled over onto the cinder track around the pitch – a small foretaste of what was to come two years later. The idea of making such a game all-ticket seems never to have occurred.

His Majesty King George V arrives at Stamford Bridge in the Royal Car. The first Royal cars were Daimlers and it was some considerable time before these were replaced with Rolls Royces.

The King, together with the Duke of York, is introduced to the Tottenham players. This was only the second Final attended by the monarch, the first having been in 1914. Despite the atrocious weather the King met both teams before the game – not something he was able to do when he attended the Final two years later!

A long range view of the game in progress in terrible conditions. These may be regarded as having helped to produce a more even contest with the Wolves adapting better than the Spurs, who had scored seventeen goals on the way to the Final but struggled to do so in the mud.

This still image from the (rare) surviving newsreel footage shows the only goal of the 1921 Final being scored by Jimmy Dimmock. The Spurs player broke through the Wolves defence and initially lost the ball before regaining possession through a lucky rebound and striking a well-placed shot past 'keeper George, who was literally floundering in the standing water on his goal-line.

Crowds swarm across the Stamford Bridge pitch after the final whistle in 1921. What is now an offence was then something of a tradition, with people keen to get a good view of the presentation. Given the conditions, this stampede must have finished the pitch off!

The King presents the trophy to Spurs captain Grimsdell. Spurs had only been back in Division One that season. Their only previous victory had been as a Southern League side, exactly twenty years earlier: the remarkable link between Spurs and a year ending in one was growing.

Arthur Grimsdell poses outside the ground with the trophy and some fans. Rather like Neville Southall in the modern game, Grimsdell was not keen on post-match celebrations and simply went off home after the photograph. Note the headgear worn by all but one in the picture.

The Tottenham Hotspur side that won the FA Cup in 1921. From left to right (players only), back row: Clay, Smith, Hunter, Walters, McDonald. Front row: Banks, Seed, Grimsdell, Cantrell, Bliss, Dimmock. Having been champions of Division Two the previous season, they finished as runners-up to Liverpool in Division One the following one, but did not reach another Cup Final until 1961.

20

The jersey worn by Wolves outside right Tancy Lea in the 1921 Final. In fact he only wore this jersey during the first half, as the players changed into dry kit at half-time and the spare jerseys did not have the embroidered Wolves badge on them. Many teams, as with Spurs in 1921, just wore ordinary jerseys for their Cup Finals rather than special ones with badges on. It is thus all the less likely that a jersey of that sort would have survived, as it would simply have been used the following season for club games. Tancy Lea was with Wolves from 1913 until 1922 and in that time made 58 first team appearances before moving on to Bristol Rovers.

The cover for the 1922 Cup Final programme. This is the third in sequence designed by Bernard Hugh and reverts to a far more complex illustration, reminiscent of the 1920 cover. Victory remains the dominant theme, depicted drawing back a curtain to reveal a game in progress at what is meant to represent Stamford Bridge. Roses ramble up two columns, which bear the names of the participating teams: Huddersfield from the white rose county and Preston from the red. The cover price was halved to three pence, but the programme was reduced to a mere eight pages, printed for the Chelsea Football and Athletic Club by Jas Truscott of EC4.

Mr D.H. Asson, one of the linesmen in 1922, as illustrated in the programme. Asson had started out as a player and was on the books of West Bromwich Albion as a teenager. An injury ended his playing prospects so he took up refereeing in 1910 and was on the League list only two years later. Given the wasted war years, it was rapid promotion indeed to be running the line at the Cup Final in 1922. Nothing, however, could have adequately prepared him for what he would have to cope with the following year when he was chosen to referee the Final.

The Preston North End team. The photograph in the match programme is a standard team group taken at Deepdale, but these cameo portraits come from the menu for the banquet held in the team's honour in Preston. The Preston team had reached the semi-final in 1921 before going out to eventual winners Spurs. Remarkably, they met Spurs again at the same stage and same venue, Hillsborough, in 1922, this time winning 2-1 with goals from Rawlings and Roberts. Thus they reached their first Final since the glory days of their remarkable double in 1889. The Preston goalkeeper was unusual in several respects. He was an amateur, when these were becoming far fewer at football's highest level, and he was a university graduate, which was a great rarity in League football. Most unusual of all however, Mitchell wore spectacles while keeping goal!

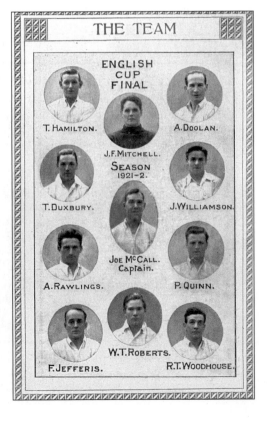

Clem Stephenson and the Huddersfield Town team at the billiard table. Media interest in the build up to major sporting events grew apace after the Great War. Players became stars off as well as on the field and photographers sought to capture the mood of a team just before a Final. Billiards was a popular activity as it lent itself to a relaxed group photograph and was something fans could easily relate to.

Huddersfield players Mutch and Watson pose having a friendly spar for the camera. Altercations at the training ground are often all too real nowadays, but in this 1922 photograph the cameraman has sought to capture a light-hearted knockabout atmosphere prior to the big game (in contrast to the almost studied formality of the billiard hall shot). Goalkeeper Mutch had been a loser in the Cup Final two years earlier.

The 1922 Final in progress, from contemporary French magazine *Le Miroir des Sports*. This clearly shows that interest in the Final had already extended overseas. Note the hoarding advertising Topical Budget newsreel footage. Such of this film as has survived provides some of our best evidence for these early Finals.

The 1922 Final was generally regarded as a dour, uncompromisingly rough affair, in fact the worst since 1904 according to some. It was decided by a controversial penalty when Hamilton cynically brought down Smith on the edge of the area and, despite widespread protest, the referee (appropriately named Fowler) gave a penalty. Mitchell, in goal, jumped about to put off the kicker but Smith coolly converted to give Huddersfield their first and, so far, only Cup Final victory.

The Huddersfield Town team with the Cup in 1922. From left to right, back row: Wood, Slade, Mutch, Wilson, Watson, Wadsworth. Front row: H. Chapman (manager), Richardson, Mann, Islip, Stephenson, Smith, J.F. Chaplin (trainer). Herbert Chapman was turning Huddersfield into the most successful side of the decade. He had emerged untainted from the fiasco involving Leeds City and he shrewdly brought Clem Stephenson to Huddersfield, as the man around whom to build his new team. Stephenson had been at Villa since 1910 and was regarded by many as past his best. Chapman had worked with Stephenson at Leeds City during the war and knew his man. It all fell into place as Huddersfield, building on their Cup success began to attract new players. In 1921/22 they finished only fourteenth in Division One. The following year they were third and for the rest of Stephenson's time with them as a player (five more years) they were never lower than second.

A glass pub sign produced by a local brewery to commemorate Huddersfield's FA Cup victory.

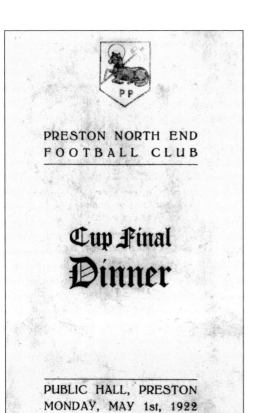

PRESTON NORTH END
FOOTBALL CLUB

Cup Final
Dinner

PUBLIC HALL, PRESTON
MONDAY, MAY 1st, 1922

The cover of the menu card from the banquet held in the Public Hall, Preston, in honour of the team's appearance in the 1922 Final. These menu cards afford quite an insight into contemporary tastes both in terms of food and also other areas of celebration. The food on offer on this occasion was very simple, wholesome English fare with no actual mention of beverages at all – though the inclusion of a drinking song in the musical programme suggests this was not a teetotal occasion! Among the toasts was one proposed by Alderman W.E. Ord JP, the first president of the club, to 'The Old Invincibles'. This was an entirely domestic occasion well away from the metropolis with none of the usual dignitaries from the FA and elsewhere in attendance. 1922 was Guild year in Preston.

Having arrived at Huddersfield station in a train specially decorated in blue and white to mark the occasion, the victorious Huddersfield Town party were taken in two corporation buses to the Town Hall for their reception. There has been, and continues to be, a great tradition of parading the cup through the streets in an open-topped vehicle – sometimes horse-drawn, but more usually motorised.

Two
The Empire Stadium

The Empire Stadium nears completion. This photograph is taken from the inside of the match programme for the 1923 Cup Final, an event which was intended to give this much vaunted new stadium a memorable inauguration. The statistical details of the new stadium, together with an account of the exhibition of which it forms a part, are fulsome and highly eulogistic. How things actually turned out on that April day in 1923, clearly no one could have expected.

THE MATCH OF THE SEASON: THE F.A. CUP FINAL.

Vizard.

Jones. Jennings. Rowley. Jack. Butler.

Pym.

Nuttall. Finney. Howarth. Seddon.

J R Smith. J. Smith. (Captain)

General view of the Stadium.

Richards. Tresadern.

Henderson. Young. Ruffell. Hufton.

Watson. Crossley. Moore. Brown.

Bishop. G. Kay. (Captain) H. D. Asson (Referee)

READY FOR THE GREAT MATCH AT WEMBLEY: THE NEW STADIUM AND THE TEAMS.

the new Stadium at Wembley, with accommodation for 125,000 spectators, London has an arena worthy of so great a sporting ccasion as the final tie for the Football Association Cup. Metropolitan interest is specially keen owing to West Ham United's having nexpectedly won their way to the final, in which they oppose the Bolton Wanderers. The upper portraits are of some Bolton players the lower ones of the men from West Ham. The identity of the actual teams to play is not known at the time of going to press. A portrait of Mr. H. D. Asson, the referee, is also given.

This whole page from the contemporary magazine, *Illustrated Sporting and Dramatic News* provided fans with a convenient preview of the big game in 1923. The news certainly turned out to be both sporting and dramatic!

This contemporary advertisement suggested that travel to the ground would be easy and convenient though hardly cheap. Getting the crowds to the stadium, then as now, was a major logistical problem. In the programme was confident mention of, 'vastly improved communications', and excursions running to Wembley from, 'all parts of the kingdom'. Every effort would seem to have been made to facilitate travel to the stadium. The same could not be said for arrangements to admit all those fans who took advantage of this wonderful transport system.

A match ticket for the first Wembley Cup Final of 1923. At fifteen shillings this represents a very expensive seat price, given that season tickets for many major clubs could be had for only three or four pounds. Tickets were only printed for a minority of the accommodation, it being assumed that with a capacity calculated at 125,000, bigger even than the Crystal Palace, there would be no problem coping with the crowds paying on the day.

Left: The front cover of the 1923 Cup Final programme. This is the most famous and, often, most sought after, but not the rarest Wembley programme. Despite its small page size, it is a substantial item at twenty-eight pages with a full colour outer cover. This was a great improvement in value from the previous year, given that the cover price remained at three pence. The number of advertisements must have helped keep the price down. There are many of these, including the remarkable Pinnace Stone Age footballers on the inside back page. In 1922 the programme had no advertising at all, but from 1923 it was there to stay. This first Wembley programme was the only one produced by W.H. Smith, at their Auden press. This firm had regularly produced unofficial souvenirs for the Crystal Palace Finals.

Below: A pirate programme for the 1923 Cup Final. It is inevitable that a major sporting event will attract those who see in it the opportunity to make easy money. In this case the pirate programme provides the barest of details and is wholly inferior to the official issue. Presumably enough fans knew no better for it to be worthwhile producing and selling these things. They continued to be a feature at big games for quite some time.

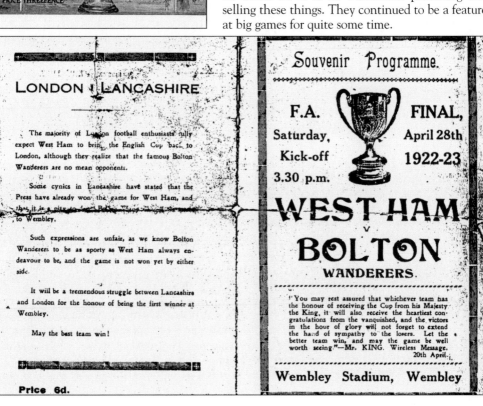

Portraits of the officials of the Football Association from inside the match programme. The president, John Charles Clegg, a solicitor from Sheffield, was one of the giants of the early game. He played in the very first international in 1872, refereed the 1882 and 1892 Finals and served on the FA committee from 1885, rising to be president from 1923 until his death in 1937. He was, in 1927, the first man to be knighted for his services to football.

F.J. Wall was similarly knighted in 1931. As paid secretary from 1895, he had seen football undergo dramatic changes by the time he handed over to his young successor in 1934.

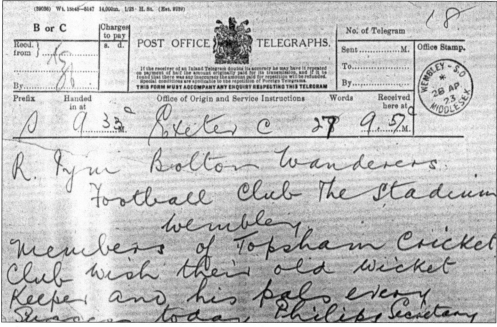

Telegrams were a popular method of effective delivery of a brief message right to the hand of an intended recipient. Many players received telegrams from friends, family, former clubs and the like just before a big game. This is the telegram to Dick Pym, Bolton's goalkeeper, from his team-mates at Topsham Cricket Club. Not surprisingly for a goalkeeper, he was also their wicketkeeper.

A photograph of the young Dick Pym wearing his 1923 Cup Final jersey. Pym had played many games for Exeter City in the Southern League and then Division Three of the Football League before his transfer to Bolton in 1921 for a record fee of around £5,000. That was money well spent as he went on to make 336 appearances for Wanderers, including three in Cup Finals. He represented both England and the Football League. Pym kept the badges from his jerseys, but wore out the jerseys themselves on nocturnal fishing trips in the Exe estuary.

A photograph of what looks like a serious road accident. This appears in the *Sunday Pictorial* the day after the 1923 Final. A motor bus overturned near Kennington Oval, the scene of the earliest Finals, while taking a party of thirty-four from Greenwich to Wembley. No one was killed, although eight were injured.

From the same newspaper came this picture of police going to Wembley by van after a desperate call for reinforcements. This was not to deal with any trouble but simply to help cope with the sheer numbers which threatened to overwhelm the stadium. Even with such reinforcements as were able to get through to the ground, the police were all but helpless in the face of a vast human tide.

Attempts to close the gates because the ground was full proved pointless as the fans simply clambered over the locked turnstiles and anywhere else they could find to gain access. Basic admission charge for standing on the terraces was two shillings, 'including tax'. As usual on such occasion, virtually everyone present wore a hat.

The build-up of crowds at another block of turnstiles. What had seemed ample turnstile provisions proved totally inadequate for the numbers that came. The ease with which turnstiles could be surmounted by the thousands who were determined to get in, having been encouraged to come, necessitated significant structural alterations before the next Final. Despite the enormous crowds and the inevitable chaos, things seem to have remained largely good-natured. Many, however, did not content themselves with simply climbing into the stadium as such, but went on to fill up the seating area – which had been the only part of the stadium for which there had been tickets printed. Those spectators who had tickets were very lucky if they could reach the seat that they had actually paid for!

In sharp contrast to the bedlam they would encounter when they got to Wembley, the Bolton players pose for a 'chorus line' style picture looking very dapper in the streets of Harrow.

Another study in pre-match relaxation, again round the billiard table. The Bolton players, with immaculately groomed hair, look totally focused on the wide expanse of green baize. As he was to do so very well in the game, young Dick Pym, (with a cue over his left shoulder) keeps his eye on the ball!

In stark contrast there was little enough green visible at Wembley as the Bolton players tried to make their way out onto the pitch, which by then was almost totally covered with spectators.

A view from the air showing the stadium full, more still making their way in and, of course, a great many spectators forced onto the pitch by the build-up of numbers. Slowly but surely, however, the field of play is being cleared in an attempt to make play possible.

A Red Cross man looks forlorn in the face of potential catastrophe. Contemporary reports mention almost a thousand casualties, mostly minor, but there were some broken bones and other more serious injuries, and some sixty people in all were taken to hospital.

The players of both sides look increasingly fed up as the climax to their season seems certain to be aborted by the problems caused by crowds on the pitch. It was, however, realised that a patient and largely good-natured crowd could not be relied upon to remain so if the game were called off.

One of the most abiding images of the 1923 Final is that of mounted PC George Scorey on his white horse Billy. Indeed this occasion is often referred to as the 'White Horse Final'. Of course there were numerous other mounted police doing sterling work to coax back the crowds, but Billy caught the eye and thus the imagination, because he was white. Horses may be seen galloping across the pitch as the captains finally shake hands, on the newsreel footage.

An unusual action shot from the Final, showing opposing centre halves Seddon and Kay going up for a high ball. The crowd forming a human touchline may be seen in the background of the picture. Seddon played in two more Finals with Bolton, being their captain in 1929. In later life he was coach with various clubs, including Liverpool (a position he held from 1936 until 1951). In 1950 he took the Merseyside team to a Wembley Cup Final, although by this time he was quite a sick man. Then, as in 1923, he experienced defeat.

After only a few moments play Bolton's elegant inside right scored the very first goal in the Empire Stadium and put Bolton on the way to victory. Bolton-born David Jack had begun his career with Plymouth Argyle. Despite the attention of London clubs he moved back to the Wanderers with whom he won two medals before being transferred to Arsenal for a record fee.

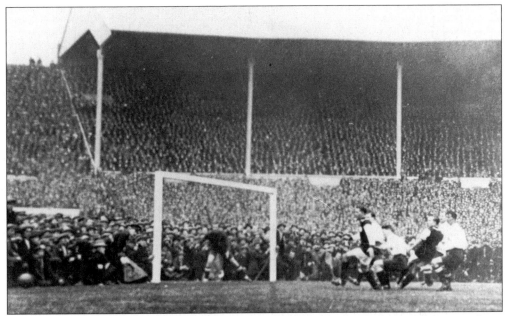

Crowds behind the goal pressed right up to the line. Netting had long since been torn down and for corners to be taken the police had to force a space clear. In the case of Bolton's second goal, scored by Smith, the ball crossed the line but bounced back from the crowd into play. Mr Asson, who had been linesman at the previous Final, gave the goal. Bolton, of course, had two players called Smith in the team – both with the initial 'J'. The scorer of this goal was centre forward J.R. Smith, who played again in the 1926 Final. He ended his career as a trainer at Cardiff City in 1939 when they were managed by former Bolton colleague Billy Jennings.

West Ham inside left Billy Moore bearing down on goal. Moore was from the tiny pit village of Seaton Delaval, which also produced Harry Wake (who would figure in the 1925 Final). He was a great servant of the Hammers, having joined them in 1922 and remaining with them as player and trainer until 1960.

Dick Pym said he was never nervous about playing at Wembley. He certainly dominated his goalmouth and, despite the problems caused by the proximity of the crowds, kept the first of his three clean sheets. Bolton had scored very early on in the game, but contemporary accounts praised West Ham for 'making the contest interesting and never ceasing to try and discover a weakness in the Bolton rearguard'. West Ham came close to scoring more than once, but Bolton had what many thought was a legitimate goal disallowed for offside. West Ham started the second half brightly, but once Bolton scored their second the result was no longer in doubt and the Hammers were a beaten team.

King George presents the Cup to Bolton captain Smith at the end of a remarkable afternoon. The arrival of the King had been a calming influence on the crowd and his presence helped to ensure that the game went ahead. Contemporary reports comment on the King's concern as more and more casualties were taken to the first-aid post in the arches just below the Royal Box.

A picture of the Bolton players outside Wembley with the FA Cup and a fierce looking mascot. The wives are rather squeezed out at the back of the group.

The official team group with the trophy, taken back at Burnden Park. From left to right, back row: G. Eccles, Nuttall, Haworth, Seddon, Pym, Jennings, Rowley, C.E. Foweraker (manager). Front row: Butler, Jack, J.R. Smith, Joe Smith, Vizard, Finney.

The jersey worn by Alex Finney, the youngest player on the Bolton side of 1923. He had been spotted while playing in a junior final at Burnden Park and he formed a natural partnership with the other full-back, Bob Haworth. Despite missing the 1926 Final through injury, by 1937 he had played 530 games for Bolton.

Dick Pym junior, himself a goalkeeper, proudly holds his father's winners medal and gold watch from the 1923 Final. Bonus payments, like the basic wages, were strictly controlled in those days, regardless of the number of paying spectators. As gifts from the club to mark their victory in the first Wembley Final, all the Bolton players were given gold watches.

The cover of the menu card from the dinner held after Bolton's historic victory in 1923. Bolton always went to the Hotel Russell on these occasions and regular finalists tended to have their favourite places for these dinners. The menu was very much French cuisine, lavish at nine courses and vastly more exotic than the one at Preston had been the previous year. The entertainment, amid the usual toasts, was a selection of songs by Miss Margaret Jewell.

Bolton Wanderers F. & A. C. Ltd.

DINNER

to celebrate the occasion of the first victory of Bolton Wanderers in the English Cup. This being the first match played on the Wembley Park Stadium Ground.

BOLTON WANDERERS

VERSUS

WEST HAM UNITED

April 28th, 1923.

J. W. MAKANT. Esq. J.P.

(President of Bolton Wanderers F. & A. C. Ltd.)

IN THE CHAIR.

HOTEL RUSSELL, LONDON.

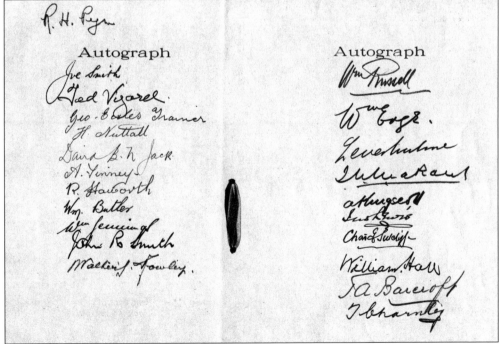

The whole central section of this menu was given over to autographs and here, on the left side, are those of the Bolton team and Eccles, the trainer. On the right are signatures of guests, including Charles Sutcliffe of the Football League, FA treasurer Kingscott and the Bolton directors.

> Spectators will have a fine view of the game from all points in the Stadium. They are earnestly requested to " pass right down the car " and, by squeezing as close as possible to their next-door neighbours in the standing enclosure, to give as many as possible of their fellow-enthusiasts a chance of fitting in and seeing the match.

In the light of all that happened that afternoon, these words from the match programme seem rather optimistic and naïve. No doubt all would have been well (and this advice appropriate) had not so many turned up to see the game. Press reports the following day said, 'The FA disclaim responsibility for the arrangements which were in the hands of the stadium authorities'.

The Football Association Challenge Cup Competition.

7I

FINAL TIE.

BOLTON WANDERERS v. WEST HAM UNITED,
Saturday, 28th April, 1923.

Under the Agreement between The Football Association and the British Empire Exhibition, the arrangements for the Sale of Tickets for Admission to the Stadium, the Provision of Police, and Control of the Ground generally, were in the hands of the British Empire Exhibition.

The Football Association deeply regrets the incidents and inconvenience caused to the Public, and will, upon production of any Tickets with Counterfoil attached, return the cost to holders who travelled to the Stadium and were prevented from taking their seats.

The Tickets, with Counterfoil attached, should be sent under cover of a letter, with stamped addressed envelope, to "Final Tie," The Football Association, 42, Russell Square, London, W.C. 1, before Monday, 14th May, 1923.

Secretary.

2, RUSSELL SQUARE,
LONDON, W.C. 1.
4th May, 1923.

An FA minute relating to the 1923 Cup Final. While accepting no responsibility for what had happened, the FA expressed regret and offered to return money to those who sent in their tickets together with counterfoils.

The Football Association Challenge Cup Competition.

FINAL TIE.

BOLTON WANDERERS v. WEST HAM UNITED,

Saturday, 28th April, 1923.

REPORT OF THE FINANCE COMMITTEE.

Upwards of 5,000 applications have been received for the return of the cost to holders of tickets who travelled to the Stadium and were prevented from taking their seats.

The number of tickets with counterfoil attached received in accordance with the offer of the 4th May represents upwards of 12,000 tickets and an amount of upwards of £4,100.

It is proposed to make all repayments by cheque.

42, RUSSELL SQUARE,
      LONDON, W.C. 1.
    28th May, 1923.

72

Another FA minute which records the remarkable number of people who were in a position to return their tickets, complete with the required counterfoils, to receive their refunds. As there were no empty seats on the day it must be assumed that they were simply filled up by anyone who could climb into them. This necessitated changes to the layout of the ground before the next game.

The Football Association Challenge Cup Competition.

FINAL TIE.

BOLTON WANDERERS v. WEST HAM UNITED,
28th April, 1923.

Report of the Ground Committee (Messrs. A. Kingscott, A. Davis, H. J. Huband, H. A. Porter, J. McKenna, J. Lewis, and T. Thorne) Supplementary to the Minutes, and the Report of the Finance Committee of the 17th May, 1923.

The Notice published on the 4th May, 1923, was approved before publication by the Emergency Committee.

The Ground Committee are in communication with the Authorities of the British Empire Exhibition.

A Meeting of the Joint Committee was held at the Stadium on Friday, the 25th May. The Ground Committee devoted the whole of the morning to inspecting the Stadium, and met the British Empire Exhibition Committee in the afternoon.

Various suggestions were made for structural alterations to the Stadium.

The following suggestions of the Ground Committee were favourably considered :—

That the Stadium be encircled that it may be a self-contained structure.

Provision to be made for feeding the terraces from the top in addition to the present entrances.

The terraces to be divided into sections, each section to be a self-contained area. Each entrance to feed its own section.

An unclimbable fence to be erected between the terraces and the stands.

The temporary seats in the ring to be dispensed with.

That gates be erected at the King's entrance and the entrance to the running track.

The turnstiles to be replaced by up-to-date stiles, and effective crush barriers to be provided.

Iron railings to be erected dividing each section of the seats in the stands.

Gates or stiles to be erected at the entrance to the staircases on the ground level of the North Stands.

Various other suggestions were made and are to be considered, and in due course the Committee will make a further report.

42, RUSSELL SQUARE,
LONDON, W.C. 1.
28th May, 1923.

A third FA minute which comments on the way forward for the next Final and shows that even after what had happened in 1923 there were those who were reluctant to embrace the concept of all-ticket matches, especially with tickets being sold in advance.

Three

The Welsh Challenge

FINAL TIE

Of the Football Association English Cup Competition

APRIL 25th, 1925

The cover of the 1925 Cup Final programme – one of the dullest of all the Wembley Final programmes, unrelieved by either colour or interesting design. Even what is quite a promising photograph of the approach to the twin towers is rendered almost invisible by the lack of contrast, all so very different from the striking colour scheme of the previous year. The teams involved in 1925 were long-established past winners Sheffield United and relative new boys Cardiff City, who were attempting to take the cup out of England for the first time.

"Bovril keeps you going"

The back page of the 1925 programme is somewhat more telling in its impact on the eye than the front. From the first Wembley programme onwards, advertising had been a major feature and its range and diversity repays study by those interested in the social history of the period. Bovril was a particularly prolific advertiser in several issues, though not always in such a prominent position. In those more innocent days, one suspects no hint of double entendre from the juxtaposition of the man in pyjamas and the slogan beneath!

A match ticket from the 1925 Final. After two issues of oblong tickets, this new shape persisted until recent times. The stadium retains its original name (Empire Stadium) on the ticket, although it makes no mention of the teams actually playing. The engraving is complex enough to deter forgery, especially in the days long before colour photocopying. In this case, the ticket was for access to the standing area behind the goal and was priced at only two shillings – including tax!

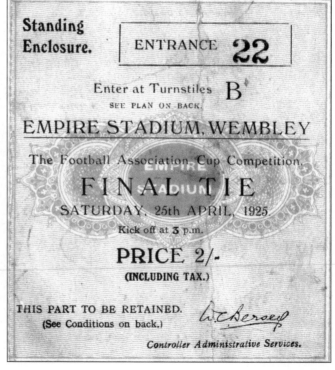

Standing Enclosure. ENTRANCE 22

Enter at Turnstiles B
SEE PLAN ON BACK.

EMPIRE STADIUM, WEMBLEY

The Football Association Cup Competition.

FINAL TIE

SATURDAY, 25th APRIL, 1925

Kick off at 3 p.m.

PRICE 2/-
(INCLUDING TAX.)

THIS PART TO BE RETAINED.
(See Conditions on back.)

Controller Administrative Services.

The Sheffield United and Cardiff City teams line up for the pre-match presentation in 1925. Cardiff had taken three games to knock out Darlington, champions of Division Three (North), but had only conceded two goals in seven games to reach the final. Sheffield had also conceded a mere two goals (to neighbours Wednesday) on their way to Wembley, and had defeated the amateur giants Corinthians 5-0.

Action from the 1925 Cup Final.

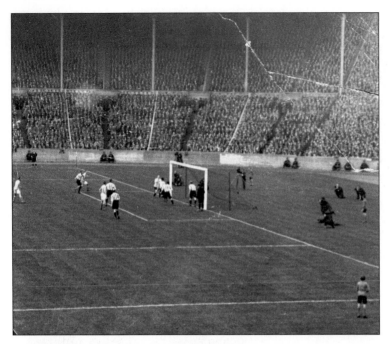

Another action shot from the 1925 Cup Final. Note the paucity of cameramen when compared with situation at a modern final.

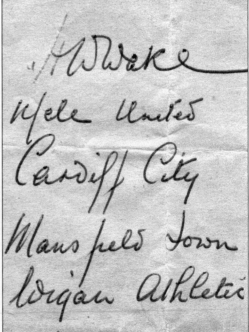

A portrait and autograph of Cardiff City right half Harry Wake. Wake was capped for England as a schoolboy from Seaton Delaval and first played League football for nearby Newcastle, in whose strip he appears here. In a tight game of two good defences, Wake made the error – failing to cut out a pass to Tunstall – which led to the only goal, defeat for the Welsh team and a fourth Cup Final victory for Sheffield.

The Duke of York, not inappropriately,
presents the trophy to the men from
Yorkshire, and medals to the Cardiff
players. For them it was still a great
achievement as they had only come into
the League in 1920, being promoted to
Division One at the first attempt; and had
come within a whisker of the
Championship itself the year before this
final. Note that it is a Cardiff player who
has the ball.

The jersey worn in the 1925 Final by Joe
Nicholson, the Cardiff centre forward.
Nicholson had joined Cardiff from
Clapton Orient as a wing half but injury
to regular striker Len Davies gave
Nicholson a chance to show he could
attack as well as defend. The programme
notes rather quaintly describe him as, 'not
a nice sort of fellow for a centre half to
have to deal with for an hour and a half'.

This attractive item is a silver cigarette case, commissioned by a local Cardiff newspaper for presentation to the City players. On one surface (above) is a lovely coloured enamel depiction of the Empire Stadium with the crest of Cardiff above it. On the other surface (below) is the inscription, 'To commemorate an honourable achievement, Wembley 25th April 1925, English Cup Final, Cardiff City v Sheffield United. Presented to Charles V. Maddox by Joe Nicholson, "a good winner and a good loser"'. Nicholson gave this item, together with his jersey, to his great friend Maddox.

The victorious Sheffield United team in 1925. This was the fiftieth FA Cup Final and Sheffield won it in a season which saw them play their one hundredth FA Cup tie, as well as their 1,000th Division One game. For them there was one more Cup Final to come but, as yet, no further victory. From left to right (players only), back row: Pantling, King, Cook, Sutcliffe, Milton, Green. Middle row: Boyle, Johnson, Gillespie. Front row: Mercer, Tunstall.

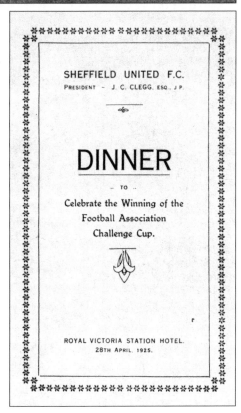

SHEFFIELD UNITED F.C.

PRESIDENT - J. C. CLEGG, ESQ., J P.

DINNER

.. TO ..

Celebrate the Winning of the
Football Association
Challenge Cup.

ROYAL VICTORIA STATION HOTEL.
28TH APRIL. 1925.

The menu cover from the dinner in celebration of the Sheffield United victory of 1925. This was a small menu card for an event at the Royal Victoria Station Hotel, almost austere in appearance. A hint of humour has crept into the list of dishes on offer, however, with the second course being, 'Clear Bramall Lane, with Creme Wembley' and, later on in the meal, a dish called 'Sheffield United Pudding'.

The cover of the 1927 Cup Final programme, for the game between Cardiff City and Arsenal. After several years of being printed and published by the Fleetway Press of Dane Street, WC1, the programmes for 1927 were produced by Fred Blower of High Street, Watford. This resulted in a back page in black and white but a cover page in very gaudy team colours of red and blue. Prophetically, perhaps, blue was the predominant colour. Advertising had by now found its way onto the actual front of the programme. This basic cover design continued in use for some time on club programmes, such as those of Queens Park Rangers.

Arsenal players warming up at Highbury the day before the game. Although it was the Gunners' first Cup Final compared to Cardiff's second, led by their very experienced captain Charles Buchan they were clear favourites to win. Buchan was to figure in numerous subsequent final programmes as a respected sports journalist.

A contemporary caricature of Arsenal captain Buchan. Born in Plumstead, he had begun his career with Arsenal but made his name with Sunderland, with whom he won a Championship and FA Cup runners-up medal. Arsenal bought him in 1925 and part of his fee was £100 for every goal he scored in his first season. To more modern fans he is perhaps best known for founding the popular magazine *Football Monthly*.

A group of lucky Cardiff City fans who had got tickets and travelled down to London for the 1927 Final. Note the rosettes, rattles and ubiquitous hats.

A very great many more Cardiff fans who did not have tickets anxiously followed the fortunes of their team by listening to the radio commentary being relayed through loud speakers in Cathays Park, Cardiff. This was the first season in which the BBC broadcast coverage of matches.

The programme of music from the 1927 Cup Final programme. This was the first final at which there was organised community singing; arranged by the *Daily Express* National Community Singing Movement. Song sheets were distributed free to all those who attended the game, thus starting a tradition which would last until quite recently.

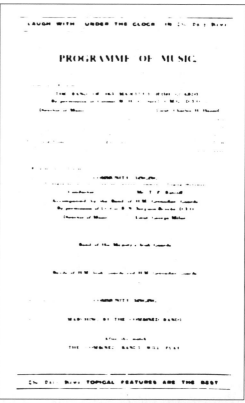

The man who led the community singing on this first occasion and thereafter for many years – and who became synonymous with it – was Mr T.P. Ratcliff, seen here high on his podium, band behind him, conducting the crowd.

King George meets the Arsenal players before the 1927 Final. Arsenal still preferred the lace-up jerseys.

Fred Keenor introduces the King to his Cardiff City team. Cardiff, as they had done two years earlier, wore jerseys with rounded necks, even though the Welsh national side continued to wear the lace-up jerseys for some years after this. It is interesting to note how some players preferred to wear their jerseys outside their shorts and some inside.

The two captains, Buchan and Keenor, meet with referee Bunnell for the toss-up before the 1927 Final. The dapper Mr Bunnell, from Lancashire, shown here wearing jacket and bow tie, is illustrated in the match programme but given no write-up at all – a far cry from earlier programmes which gave full pen pictures of all three officials.

Because of the historic nature of the victory, scenes from the 1927 Final figured on many cigarette cards. This one shows Keenor, the Cardiff captain, in action.

A tussle in the Cardiff City goalmouth during the 1927 Cup Final. It is almost a case of 'spot the ball'.

More action in front of the Cardiff goal as Arsenal skipper Buchan and Cardiff's Hardy go up together for a ball in the air. Hardy, a Northumbrian, was very distinctive because of his bald head, rather like the contemporary Welsh international Moses Russell.

Yet more pressure on the Cardiff goal in as Hardy clears another Arsenal attack. Hardy was regarded by many as the best player on the field in a fairly dour game and he certainly played a key role in neutralising much of the Gunners' firepower.

Buchan tests Farquharson in the Cardiff goal. The Arsenal captain was, arguably, the only one on his side – which was still in the process of being built up by the new manager Herbert Chapman – who lived up to his reputation. He created several good chances for his colleagues but a winners medal was to elude his grasp again. He was too old to figure in Chapman's longer-term plans, which were to reap such rich rewards.

As in 1925, the 1927 Final turned on a mistake and was decided by a single goal. Two years earlier it had been a Cardiff error but this time a Welshman, Dan Lewis, playing in goal for Arsenal, made the slip which allowed Cardiff to take the FA Cup out of England for the first, and so far the only, time. This picture shows the first phase of Lewis' fumble.

The fumble at a more advanced stage. What had seemed a somewhat speculative shot in the 73rd minute by Ferguson from outside the area was to prove decisive. As Len Davies raced in looking for a rebound, the Arsenal 'keeper lost his concentration and with it his grasp on a ball he would normally have taken comfortably. It slipped away from him and, despite his flailing efforts to recover, rolled into the net.

Cardiff City's best player in the 1927 Cup Final, Billy Hardy, looking older than his thirty-six years, is assisted by police in making his way through crowds of jubilant Blues fans towards the steps up to the Royal Box.

Looking more than a little satisfied, Cardiff skipper Keenor cradles the Cup as he descends from the Royal Box. He had kept his promise to come back, make amends for 1925 and finally take the Cup out of England. The 'English' Cup was no longer a suitable name for the trophy.

The Cardiff fans in the stadium were elated by their unexpected piece of good fortune when Ferguson scored, not least among them being one of Wales' most famous sons, the former prime minister David Lloyd George, seen here celebrating in the Royal Box.

The crowds that had listened to the radio commentary were as nothing compared to the vast numbers who gathered to welcome Fred Keenor and his heroes bringing what had always been referred to as the 'English Cup' back to Wales. The triumphant drive through Cardiff in an open brake was seen by a crowd of over 250,000.

The victorious Cardiff City team of 1927 with the trophy.

A group of items of memorabilia relating to the 1927 Final, including the jersey worn by Len Davies – whose predatory menace at a crucial time had played a vital, and often underrated, part in the decisive goal. Also here is the medal and jersey of the youngster Ernie Curtis. At nineteen, he had only made his first team debut a few months earlier and was now brought in to replace the luckless Harry Wake who was injured just before the final. Towards the end of the game Curtis had a good chance to put the game beyond doubt but missed.

Two old adversaries and friends reminisce looking at a 1927 Cup Final programme beneath a picture of the fateful goal. Fred Keenor of Cardiff and Bob John of Arsenal were on opposite sides that day in 1927 but played together many times for Wales. John was to go on and win a great many honours with the wonderful Arsenal side that Herbert Chapman created to dominate the 1930s and eventually retired in 1938 having played 521 times for the Gunners. In that same year, 1938, poor Fred Keenor, who had finished playing for Cardiff in 1931, became dangerously ill and notices went into the Cardiff programmes asking for funds to help him and his family through their crisis. He pulled through and survived until 1971.

Four

Transition

An advertisement for the 1924 Cup Final. The final of 1923 had been, at best, a triumph of patient co-operation over chaos. What could so easily have been a major disaster became the stuff of legend. It could not, however, be allowed to happen again. A great deal of discussion went on in FA Council meetings about changes necessitated by a shambles for which they disclaimed any responsibility. Among many points of interest in FA minutes is the remarkable comment that the turnstiles 'used at the Cup Final were of an obsolete nature'. This sits ill with the image presented of the stadium before that first match, but the minute goes on to record that 'their use had represented a very material economy in expenditure'. Eventually it was agreed what changes needed to be made 'to avoid a repetition of the incidents of the match of 1923'. One point of dispute between the FA and the Exhibition Authorities was that, having decided to make finals all-ticket, they couldn't agree whether or not to sell tickets on the day. The FA were reluctant to countenance extensive advance sales to prevent 'their getting into the hands of speculators, and to forgery'. In the end the FA gave in on the grounds that 'responsibility for making suitable arrangements', rested with the Exhibition Authorities.

The striking cover of the 1924 Cup Final programme. The very unusual artwork and colouring (which appears to show Aston Villa playing Sunderland rather than Newcastle) makes this a particularly attractive programme. Page size was increased from the tiny 7' x 5' of 1923 to 10' x 7', but the cover price rocketed fourfold to the 'astronomical' sum of a shilling. This meant that the programme cost half as much as the admission price. Few were sold, of which many rapidly lost their flimsy outer covers on a wet afternoon. These factors make this (by far) the rarest of all Wembley Cup Final programmes.

Two extrovert Newcastle fans sporting giant bow ties. Magpies fans had further to travel than most for their Cup Finals, but the train service was good and the pilgrimage to the metropolis had become an established occurrence during the Edwardian era, when United had played in no less than five finals at the Crystal Palace.

Action from the 1924 Final as Harris of Newcastle is being checked by Mort of Villa while Smart (on the ground) looks on. In 1913 Villa player Stephenson had an eve-of-final dream which correctly foretold the result. In 1924 it was Harris of United who had predicted in the press before the game that Villa would be beaten by two goals, as indeed happened.

As extra-time began to look increasingly likely and Harris' prediction correspondingly unlikely, the Newcastle centre forward himself broke through to shock Villa with a late goal. The contemporary newspaper accounts were somewhat extreme – 'Wembley-Woe, Wet and Wobble' ran one headline, 'Aston Villa thrashed after having much the bigger of the play in the wettest final in history. Newcastle individualism prevails over Villa's combination'. Perhaps the oddest headline is that which read 'Ugh! Sensational finish to the Cup Final: Two goals for "Geordies" in four minutes: Ugh!'

A few days before this game Villa had defeated Newcastle 6-1 in a League match. That they could not repeat such a score in the Cup Final was in great measure due to the heroics of reserve 'keeper Bradley who had been drafted in at the last minute to replace Mutch (denying him a third final in five years).

United skipper Frank Hudspeth looks rather gingerly at the trophy as the Duke of York presents it to him in 1924. This result neatly reversed that of United's first-ever Cup Final in 1905 when they lost 0-2 to Villa at the start of their frequent but ill-starred visits to the Crystal Palace. The cameo portraits are of the goalscorers Harris (bottom left) and Seymour (top right).

Hudspeth chatting to a caped constable on his way to the Royal Box.

Newcastle captain Hudspeth, now looking more relaxed, carries the Cup off down the players' tunnel and is greeted with handshakes from happy fans. One of the linesmen may be seen in the background. This picture perfectly captures the atmosphere of what was a friendly and wet occasion.

The Newcastle United 1924 Cup-winning team. After such unfortunate experiences in five Crystal Palace finals, United clearly found Wembley very much more to their liking. However, their road to this Cup Final had been by no means easy. Villa had swept through all their games scoring fifteen goals and conceding only one to Newcastle's neighbours, lowly Ashington, whereas Newcastle had fought an epic battle with Derby County before eventually winning 5-3 in a third replay. In the semi-final United had defeated Manchester City in the last game in the long and distinguished career of the great Billy Meredith.

The FA Cup outside Bob McKenzie's shop in Blyth. It used to be quite the fashion for the trophy to go on display in various shops in the vicinity of their holders so that the public at large could see it. Despite the notorious incident at Shillcock's in Birmingham in 1895, this practice continued until well after the Second World War.

73

The cover of the 1926 Cup Final programme. Fleetway Press produced this issue with quite a lively and attractive design, although the players appear to be in action in the car park. For some reason the artwork for these programmes featured the old fashioned button-ended balls long after they had ceased being used on the field of play.

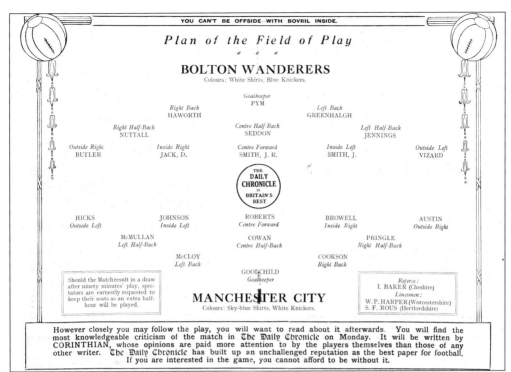

Plan of the Field of Play

BOLTON WANDERERS
Colours: White Shirts, Blue Knickers.

Goalkeeper
PYM

Right Back   *Left Back*
HAWORTH   GREENHALGH

Right Half-Back   *Centre Half-Back*   *Left Half-Back*
NUTTALL   SEDDON   JENNINGS

Outside Right   *Inside Right*   *Centre Forward*   *Inside Left*   *Outside Left*
BUTLER   JACK, D.   SMITH, J. R.   SMITH, J.   VIZARD

THE
DAILY
CHRONICLE
IS
BRITAIN'S
BEST

HICKS   JOHNSON   ROBERTS   BROWELL   AUSTIN
Outside Left   *Inside Left*   *Centre Forward*   *Inside Right*   *Outside Right*

McMULLAN   COWAN   PRINGLE
Left Half-Back   *Centre Half-Back*   *Right Half-Back*

McCLOY   COOKSON
Left Back   *Right Back*

GOODCHILD
Goalkeeper

MANCHESTER CITY
Colours: Sky-blue Shirts, White Knickers.

Should the Match result in a draw after ninety minutes' play, spectators are earnestly requested to keep their seats as an extra half-hour will be played.

Referee:
I. BAKER (Cheshire)
Linesmen:
W. P. HARPER (Worcestershire)
S. F. ROUS (Hertfordshire)

However closely you may follow the play, you will want to read about it afterwards. You will find the most knowledgeable criticism of the match in The Daily Chronicle on Monday. It will be written by CORINTHIAN, whose opinions are paid more attention to by the players themselves than those of any other writer. The Daily Chronicle has built up an unchallenged reputation as the best paper for football. If you are interested in the game, you cannot afford to be without it.

The centre spread from the 1926 programme. Bolton returned largely unchanged from 1923, whilst City had not been in a Cup Final since 1904 and the days of Meredith. Note the almost subliminal Bovril advertising which appears throughout the programme. The name of one linesman should ring a bell. The former St Lukes College goalkeeper, like so many, turned to the whistle when injury prevented progress as a player. He had to climb out of college after hours to attend his referees' course, but made rapid progress and within a short time was refereeing internationals and running the line at the Cup Final.

The Manchester City team that played in the 1926 Final. Long-serving goalkeeper Jim Goodchild was probably the best City player on the day, particularly in thwarting the efforts of J.R. Smith. Charlie Pringle, the right half, was a link with the 1904 Final as he had married the great Meredith's eldest daughter Lily and ended up playing alongside his father-in-law in the City side of the early 1920s.

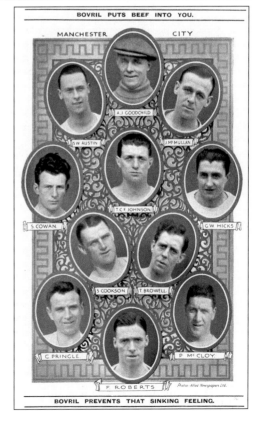

MANCHESTER CITY

A. J. GOODCHILD
S. W. AUSTIN
J. McMULLAN
T. C. F. JOHNSON
S. COWAN
G. W. HICKS
S. COOKSON
T. BROWELL
C. PRINGLE
P. McCLOY
F. ROBERTS

Photos-Allied Newspapers Ltd.

An advertisement from the 1926 programme. Both entire teams and individual players were increasingly being used to endorse a wide range of products.

The Bolton captain, with or without his Lakerol tablets, leads out his team for the 1926 Final – a very much easier operation than when he had last tried to do so three years earlier.

The 1926 Final was a game of two outstanding goalkeepers. Dick Pym, always cool and dependable, played a key role in the Bolton victory by defying every Manchester attack on his goal. Here he is in total concentration.

The victorious Bolton team with the FA Cup and the (rather larger) Lancashire Senior Cup. Just as the 1924 Final had exactly reversed the 1905 Final, so this 1926 Final reversed the results from 1904, when City had beaten Wanderers with a single goal scored by Charlie Pringle's father-in-law.

L·N·E·R

CUP FINAL

WEMBLEY

Saturday, 21st April.

ORGANISE A PARTY

AND TRAVEL

L·N·E·R

TO

WEMBLEY HILL STATION

(Nearest Station to the Stadium.)

SPECIAL FACILITIES OFFERED.

Parties desiring Saloon Accommodation should apply at once to any L.N.E.R. station or office, or to Dean & Dawson's, 53, Piccadilly, Manchester, where full particulars may be obtained.

BOOK NOW
TO AVOID DISAPPOINTMENT.

ALLIED NEWSPAPERS LIMITED, Printers, Withy Grove, Manchester.

This advertisement from the back page of a Manchester City programme is for rail travel to the 1928 Final. It appeared long before it was known which teams would actually be playing. In the event there was a Lancashire team in the Cup Final – though it wasn't City. In those days it was possible for people to write in and buy tickets for the final by post. Indeed, there are letters of complaint in some programmes from fans who couldn't get quite as many as they had asked for!

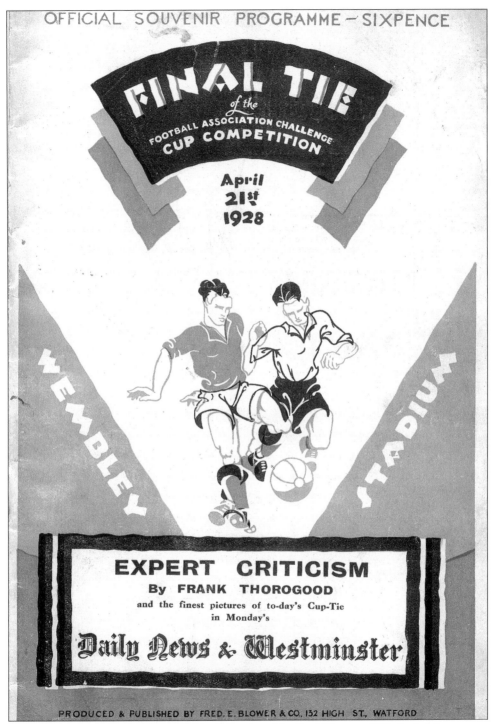

The programme cover for the 1928 Final. Produced by Fred Blower of Watford, it has a very striking and unusual colour scheme of pink, green and black on a white background in a sort of Art Deco style. Two of the inside pages also have a pink and green colour scheme, advertising wirelesses and HMV records respectively.

The Huddersfield Town team that played in the 1928 Final. Built up by Herbert Chapman, the greatest manager of his generation, the club had, since 1922, won the FA Cup, three successive League titles and a runners-up position. They went into the 1928 Final with a clear chance of the double, but failed on both accounts. With no less than five games left to play after the Cup Final, they lost three of them to finish runners-up again, two points behind Everton.

King George is presented to the Huddersfield Town team before the 1928 Final.

A close-up shot of the two 1928 Final captains, Clem Stephenson and Harry Healless, shaking hands before the game. The referee was Mr. T.G. Bryan of Willenhall. The image provides a particularly good view of the ball, showing the arrangement of the panels and, of course, the lacing.

Huddersfield had taken three games to get past Sheffield United in the semi-final but had previously brushed aside Spurs 6-1, and they were at the opposite end of the table to Rovers. Cup Finals produce shocks however, and none more quickly than when Blackburn took the lead in the very first minute. Not unlike the goal scored by another Lancashire centre forward thirty years later, Roscamp seized his opportunity and both 'keeper and ball ended up in the goal.

The King presents runners-up medals to the defeated favourites Huddersfield Town. Clem Stephenson was about to retire after a distinguished playing career filled with honours. In this, his last full season, he ended up second in both League and FA Cup competitions. He was, however, not yet finished with visits to Wembley.

A contemporary cartoon version of some of the players who would be appearing in the 1929 Final. Depicting players thus in both newspapers and magazines became increasingly popular. The features of some players, of course, lent themselves more easily than others to such treatment. These come from *All Sports Weekly* on the cover of which was a full size caricature of Fred Kean in a remarkable pose. Note the attempts at depicting stereotypical fans amongst the players.

A contemporary pen drawing of Jimmy Seddon (by the same artist who drew Buchan – see p.55). Seddon was a local boy who rose to captain his side to a Wembley victory. Originally he had been invited in his teens, while waiting at a railway station, to make up the numbers for Bolton reserves. His three Cup-winners medals and six England caps were all won despite persistent problems caused by his having contracted trench foot whilst serving in France.

An interesting crowd shot showing people receiving their song sheets, the inevitable headgear and just a few ladies. The crowd is far from being tightly packed, not surprising as only 93,000 attended the match.

Jimmy Seddon introduces the Prince of Wales to the Bolton players. Young striker Harold Blackmore looks anxiously along the line. At the end is veteran goalkeeper Dick Pym, who had played almost 500 games of senior football for at his two clubs. Note the distinctive shape of the badge for the 1929 Final, clearly shown against the dark background of Pym's jersey.

Billy Butler shielding the ball. Note the way the Portsmouth jersey has a lace-up collar with the lace actually in use, whereas the Bolton players removed the laces from their jerseys before the game. Butler, a popular man with the ladies, became popular with all Bolton fans when he opened the scoring after 78 minutes.

Dick Pym commanding his goal area. He is supported by Seddon (close to him), Haworth (on the line) and Nuttall (with his back to the camera). Referee Arnold Josephs from South Shields is in the foreground. Pym went into this game, which was his third final in seven years, nursing an injury but was still able to keep a (third) clear sheet.

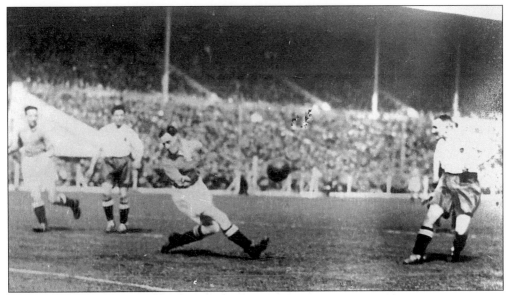

Soon after Butler had given the Trotters the lead, centre forward Harold Blackmore put the result beyond doubt with a second Bolton goal that left the Pompey defence stranded. After the controversial sale of David Jack to the Arsenal for a record fee, Blackmore, with 37 goals in 43 appearances, had helped keep the club afloat in the League after being bottom.

Jimmy Seddon and Bolton players with the FA Cup before their lap of honour. Other players in clear view are Cook, Haworth, Butler and McClelland. Note the newsreel cameraman grappling to get some close-up footage.

The victorious Bolton side of 1929 back at Burnden Park with the trophy. From left to right, back row: Kean, Haworth, Pym, Finney, Nuttall. Front row: Butler, McClelland, Seddon, Blackmore, Gibson, Cook. For almost half the team this was a third successful trip to Wembley, but things had already begun to go downhill and as more of these players retired Bolton slipped out of Division One and would not play in another Cup Final until 1953.

The grandfather clock presented to Harold Blackmore after the 1929 Final. In the FA Cup, bonus payments were strictly limited: in the first six rounds to a £2 win bonus, in the semi-final to a £4 win bonus and to £8 in the final. For a draw in any round, including the final, only a pound could be paid. In 1923 the Bolton players had been given gold watches (see p.42), in 1926 canteens of cutlery and in 1929 grandfather clocks!

Bolton's former Exeter City players Dick Pym and Harold Blackmore with the trophy back at Burnden Park. Pym had taken a Bolton side to St James' Park for a friendly and he more than anyone experienced the firepower of young Blackmore. Harold enjoyed his time at Bolton before moving to Middlesborough where he was less happy. Both men enjoyed the traditional drink from the trophy but only lemonade as both were teetotal.

EXETER CITY
v.
NEWPORT C.

on

Saturday, 22nd October, 1983

Kick-off 3.00 p.m.

PROGRAMME 40p

Canon

LEAGUE

DIVISION III

LOTTERY WINNING NUMBER for Week ending 15th October, 1983	
MONDAY	0
TUESDAY	9
WEDNESDAY	3
THURSDAY	2
FRIDAY	6

Fifty years on the same pair are together again, this time at St James' Park. This picture appeared on the front of the Exeter v. Newport programme, but was taken at the previous home game when Bolton were the visitors and by then no longer members of soccer's elite. Both these players had returned to their native Exeter when their League careers were over.

89

The Cup Tie Team, 1929

❖

"Congratulations"
and
"Better luck next time"

❖

Photo by   S. Cribb

From left to right : F. Cook, J. W. Smith, T. Bell, D. Watson,

F. Forward, J. Weddle, J. McIlwaine, D. Thackeray

J. A. Mackie, J. Nichol, J. Gilfillan.

A page from inside the menu card for the civic dinner given at Portsmouth Guildhall on Monday 6 May in honour of the 1929 runners-up. On the night of the actual game the post-match dinner had been held at the Restaurant Frascati in Oxford Street. The wish for 'Better Luck Next Time' was not fulfilled as Portsmouth took two further attempts before finally winning a Cup Final.

FINAL TIE

Of The
Football Association Challenge Cup Competition.

Official Souvenir Programme
6d

EMPIRE STADIUM, WEMBLEY
APRIL 26th 1930.

EXPERT CRITICISM
OF TO-DAY'S MATCH BY
CHARLES BUCHAN
(Famous International and Former Arsenal Captain, now on the "Daily News" Sports Staff)

IN
MONDAY'S **Daily News** FINEST PICTURES

BIG PUZZLE PRIZES - SEE BACK PAGE

PRINTED & PUBLISHED BY F.E.BLOWER & Cº 132.HIGH STREET, WATFORD

The front cover of the programme from the 1930 Final. This was the last product of Fred Blower for while and has, in a position of prominence on the front cover, the name of the Arsenal captain of just three years previously, by then a well-established sports journalist. Inside the programme some two and a half pages were devoted to advertisements for radio, a similar number were given over for tobacco products and a full page devoted to Manfield Boots (here endorsed by both managers).

The Radio Times' enables you to choose your programmes in advance

THE
RADIO TIMES
THE JOURNAL OF THE BRITISH BROADCASTING CORPORATION

NATION SHALL SPEAK PEACE UNTO NATION

| Vol. 27. No. 342. | [Registered at the G.P.O. as a Newspaper.] | APRIL 18, 1930. | Every Friday. TWO PENCE. |

ON SATURDAY, APRIL 26, BRITAIN WILL HEAR—

—A RUNNING COMMENTARY ON THE F.A. CUP FINAL

The front cover of the *Radio Times* from just before the 1930 Cup Final. Radio was rapidly growing in popularity, although sets were expensive. Echo models advertised in the programme cost £21 for a three valve set and £12 17s 6d for a two valve set – both considerable sums. This *Radio Times* cover had the Wembley pitch divided into eight segments so that the commentator could refer to where the ball was at any given moment. That commentator was George Allison, a great pioneer of radio broadcasting of football. He also had long associations with Arsenal, having reported on their games as a journalist since 1906 and having joined their board in 1926. He was to become their manager after the tragic death of Herbert Chapman.

The King meets the Huddersfield Town players before the 1930 Cup Final.

The victorious Arsenal team with the Cup. As he had previously done at Huddersfield, when he moved to become the manager of Arsenal Herbert Chapman brought in some key players to transform the Gunners from mediocrity to supremacy. In his first season he took Arsenal to their highest ever League position, runners up to his previous club Huddersfield. 1927 saw them reach their first Cup Final. With the influx of youth and experience – players like Bastin, Hapgood, James and Jack – Chapman made sure that the Arsenal would dominate the thirties. The 1930 Cup Final victory was, after forty-four years, the club's first major success. More was soon to follow.

Arsenal Football Club, Ltd.,

and

Huddersfield Town
Association Football Club, Ltd.

CUP FINALISTS
1930

Dinner and Dance

Given by the above Clubs

at the
WHARNCLIFFE ROOMS
HOTEL GREAT CENTRAL

Saturday, 26th April, 1930.

The front cover of the menu card for the post match banquet after the 1930 Final. Unusually, both the victorious Arsenal and the defeated Huddersfield teams dined together. Both sides owed so much to one man – Herbert Chapman. Even the relatively new Huddersfield manager was none other than Clem Stephenson, who had figured so prominently in Chapman's team building at Leeds Road. As the decade closed the mantle of success had shifted firmly South thanks to the greatest manager of his day.

Five

The Drift to War

The previous decade had closed with a portentous but, at that stage, harmless German aerial presence when the vast bulk of the *Graf Zeppelin* passed over Wembley during the 1930 Cup Final. There had been a rapid proliferation of wireless sets and a corresponding increase in the numbers listening to live commentaries of Cup Finals. By the end of the next decade, as technology moved on apace, there came a new medium which was to have an overwhelming impact on the game – television. Far more sinister, however, was the growing threat of another major war which would destroy, along with so much else, another generation of footballers as the first one had done. As the decade closed with the outbreak of war, the Cup went South, where it remained for seven long years. This picture is an aerial view of Wembley stadium on a toffee tin. The stadium had become the 'venue of legends' from year one and was soon sufficiently famous to attract interest as a marketing ploy.

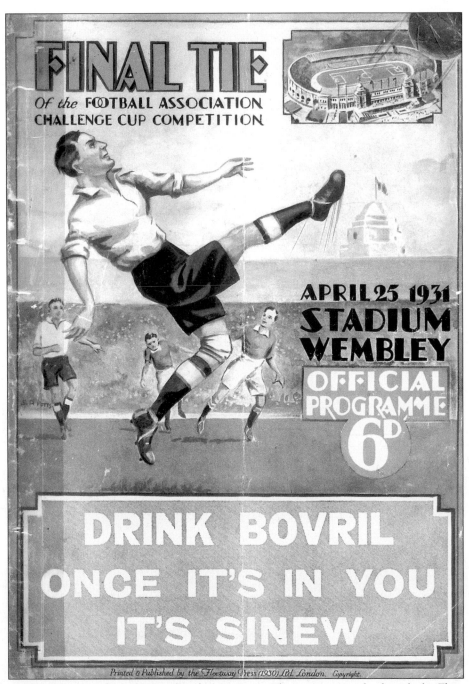

The front cover from the 1931 Cup Final programme. The contract was back with the Fleetway Press, who designed some lively and colourful artwork. Bovril now usurped the plum front page position from the *Daily News*. On the back cover is a colourful full-page advertisement for Mazda lamps. Inside the programme is another full-page advertisement for Gaumont Sound News. Not only could people see newsreel footage of the highlights in their cinema, but they could now enjoy them with sound. An unusual advertisement in the programme is for Madame Tussauds, where both captains (Barkas and Glidden) could be seen in wax!

PROGRAMME

BIRMINGHAM

V

W. BROMWICH ALBION

ENGLISH CUP FINAL

AT

WEMBLEY STADIUM

SATURDAY APRIL 25TH.

The cover of a pirate programme from the 1931 Final. In contrast to the official version this is a poor dull effort which ought to have fooled nobody. That these things were produced on such occasions, however, is clear indication that there will always be enough people who know no better to make such an enterprise worthwhile.

An informal photograph of the West Bromwich players with a Royal fan, the then Prince of Wales, who was paying a congratulatory visit. Prince Edward, later Duke of Windsor, was himself no mean soccer player and was thought by some to have deserved a place in the England amateur side.

The jersey worn in the 1931 Final by the 'baby' of the side Teddy Sandford, who was only twenty. In the official programme there is an advertisement to the effect that 'West Brom are playing today in St Margarets Jerseys'. Along with Bukta, this was one of the leading manufacturers.

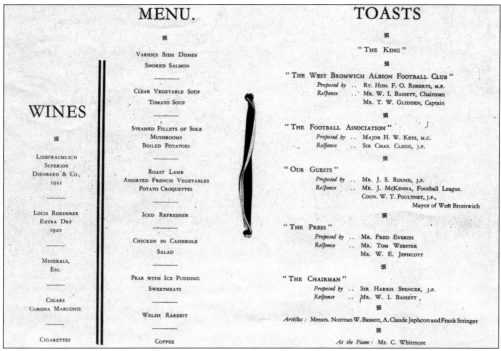

MENU.	TOASTS

MENU.

⚙

VARIOUS SIDE DISHES
SMOKED SALMON

———

CLEAR VEGETABLE SOUP
TOMATO SOUP

———

STEAMED FILLETS OF SOLE
MUSHROOMS
BOILED POTATOES

———

ROAST LAMB
ASSORTED FRENCH VEGETABLES
POTATO CROQUETTES

———

ICED REFRESHER

———

CHICKEN IN CASSEROLE
SALAD

———

PEAR WITH ICE PUDDING
SWEETMEATS

———

WELSH RAREBIT

———

COFFEE

WINES

⚙

LIEBFRAUMILCH
SUPERIOR
DIENBARD & CO.,
1921

———

LOUIS ROEDERER
EXTRA DRY
1920

———

MINERALS,
Etc.

———

CIGARS
CORONA MARCONIS

———

CIGARETTES

TOASTS

⚙

" THE KING "

⚙

" THE WEST BROMWICH ALBION FOOTBALL CLUB "
Proposed by .. RT. HON. F. O. ROBERTS, M.P.
Response ..' MR. W. I. BASSETT, Chairman
MR. T. W. GLIDDEN, Captain

⚙

" THE FOOTBALL ASSOCIATION "
Proposed by .. MAJOR H. W. KEYS, M.C.
Response .. SIR CHAS. CLEGG, J.P.

⚙

" OUR GUESTS "
Proposed by .. MR. J. S. ROUND, J.P.
Response .. MR. J. McKENNA, Football League.
COUN. W. T. POULTNEY, J.P.,
Mayor of West Bromwich

⚙

" THE PRESS "
Proposed by .. MR. FRED EVERISS
Response .. MR. TOM WEBSTER
MR. W. E. JEPHCOTT

⚙

" THE CHAIRMAN "
Proposed by .. SIR HARRIS SPENCER, J.P.
Response .. MR. W. I. BASSETT .

⚙

Artistes : Messrs. Norman W. Bassett, A. Claude Jephcott and Frank Stringer

⚙

At the Piano : Mr. C. Whitmore

The inside pages of the menu card from the WBA dinner at the Hotel Great Central after the 1931 Final. The food and drink are set out in detail but it is the extent and diversity of the toasts which catch the eye. Note the toast to 'The Press' proposed by long serving WBA secretary Everiss and replied to by Tom Webster of the wry humour and growing fame as a commentator on the newsreels. Note also the innocent use as a spacer of an ancient symbol which would all too soon come to have very far from innocent connotations.

The Albion team that won the Cup in 1931. This was to be a 'double' for the Throstles as, after winning the Cup on April 25, they went on to win their two remaining League games and thus became champions of Division Two. Over 52,000 saw the Cup paraded round the Hawthorns before the crucial final League game, in which Charlton were beaten 3-2.

A match card for the 1932 Cup Final advertising Carreras cigarettes. Unlike the pirate programmes, which were produced to make easy money, these items were distributed free to promote the product.

Captain Jimmy Nelson introduces King George to Jack Allen, the man who would go on to score such a controversial goal as an equaliser not long before half-time and tip the balance Newcastle's way. The players are, from left to right: Lang, Allan, Boyd, Richardson, McKenzie, Weaver, Davidson, McInroy, Fairhurst.

Newcastle United, winners of the FA Cup in 1932. Two years earlier, Chapman had taken Arsenal to their first victory and that was followed by their first Championship (which was also the first by any club from the South). In 1932 Arsenal had looked likely 'double' winners at one stage but after losing to Newcastle at Wembley they failed to overtake Everton in the League, despite dropping only one point in four games, and were runners-up. The Cup Final itself turned on a controversial refereeing decision: Jack Allen headed home from a cross which contemporary footage shows had almost certainly crossed the goal line before Richardson pulled it back for his centre forward.

Some famous referees – including those who officiated at the Cup Finals. Over the period in question the prominence given to match officials in the programme dwindled dramatically from portraits and biographies of all three taking up a whole page down to nothing at all other than the names on the centre page. This page from a pocket compendium of contemporary stars does something to redress the balance.

101

The 1933 Final was by no means a classic but was free from any controversy. Everton were at their peak, were expected to win and duly did so. Shown here is the jersey worn by Ernie Toseland of Manchester City. This was the first final in which numbered jerseys were worn: Everton with numbers one to eleven and City with twelve to twenty-two.

In 1933 the programme contract went back to Fred Blower and the cover has a familiar look about it with players playing in the car park and the *News Chronicle* back on the front page. It was the two very different versions of the back page *News Chronicle* advertisement that provided the only major case of variations within programmes issued for the same pre-war final. Many post-war programmes exhibit more or less minor variations and so too do the issues for 1930 and 1939. Here, however, we have two quite different versions of a cartoon by the famous cartoonist Bateman.

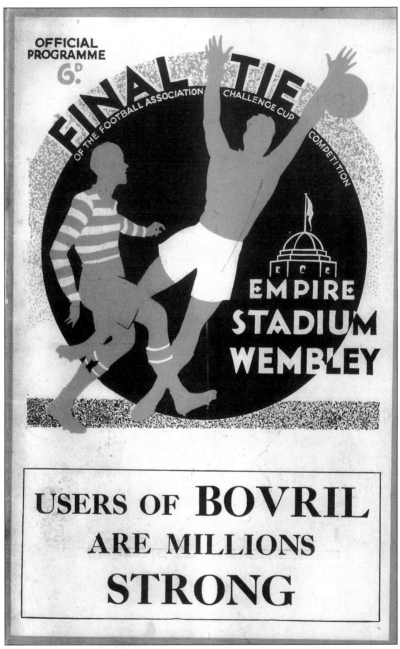

Fleetway Press were back for the 1934 programme and they retained the contract down to the war. In 1934 they produced a vivid design in red and black on white. Bovril was restored to the front cover and Mazda lamps to the back page. There were no advertisements for tobacco products but quite a few for beer, including a full-page general eulogy of its benefits. There was again no other mention of the referee other than the basic 'Referee S.F. Rous (Hertfordshire)'. This Watford schoolmaster was soon to quit his classroom forever and commit his whole life to football. Later this year he took over from Wall as secretary of the FA where one of his first jobs was to produce a definitive codification of the laws. He went on to become President of FIFA and widely known as 'Mr Football.'

L. Barnett   F. Swift   W. Dale

M. Busby   S. Cowan   J. Bray

F. Toseland   E. Brook

Manchester City
Saturday,
April 28th, 1934

R. Marshall   S. Tilson   A. Herd

The Manchester City team that returned to Wembley in 1934 to win the Cup for the first time in thirty years. The game was played in a dramatic atmosphere of thunder and lightning. Just before a half-hour had gone, Rutherford gave Pompey the lead when a speculative effort deceived teenage City 'keeper Swift. The youngster was devastated but centre forward Tilson calmed him with the promise that he himself would score two to win the match. An injury to Allen changed the pattern of the game and, true to his word, Tilson scored twice and Swift got a winners medal, having fainted when the final whistle was blown.

The Portsmouth team defeated in the 1934 Final. Only one would still be playing for them when Pompey finally won the trophy at the third attempt five years later.

The cheque for Portsmouth's share of the gate from the 1934 final, signed by FA treasurer Henry Huband.

*W*ITH fervent loyalty The Football Association congratulate His Majesty King George V upon the Silver Jubilee Year of his eventful reign, and trust that under the protection of Divine Providence he will continue to govern the United Kingdom and Empire during many years of Peace and Prosperity. The Football Association are ever mindful of the abiding interest of His Majesty in the sports and pastimes of his people and tender heartfelt thanks to their Gracious and Royal Patron.

The cover of the 1935 Cup Final programme was dominated by dazzling silver in honour of the Jubilee. This silvering accentuated any fold in the programme and as a result smooth-looking examples are scarce. This is the full-page loyal address from inside the programme. The King had attended himself in 1934, but on this occasion he was represented by the Prince of Wales (who would soon be embroiled in the abdication crisis). A portrait of Stanley Rous now joined those of FA grandees Clegg, Pickford and Huband and, maybe due to his influence, a photograph of the referee A.E. Fogg was included in the programme.

The West Bromwich Albion team for the
1935 Cup Final included no fewer than
nine of those who had defeated
Birmingham four years earlier. This was the
eighth final appearance by Albion but, in a
fast and frantic game (which saw more
goals than any other in this period), they
eventually went down to a pair of late
goals. Wednesday took the initiative with a
second minute goal from Palethorpe, but
the Albion new boy Boyes equalised with
the best goal of the game mid-way through
the first half. Hooper converted
Wednesday's growing superiority into a
lead with a goal in the 67th minute, but
Albion fought back well and Teddy
Sandford scored a fine equaliser a few
minutes later. The spectators seemed well
set to enjoy another half and hour of
entertaining football until Ellis Rimmer
seized victory for Wednesday with two
goals in the dying minutes of the game.

Sheffield Wednesday with the FA Cup in 1935. Ellis Rimmer, the outside left whose two goals
in the closing minutes killed off the Albion challenge, had scored in every round up to and now
including the final.

The Sheffield United players pose with their Shredded Wheat in a Cup Final preview newspaper in 1936. Individual players had long been used in advertising to endorse a variety of products, but by this time whole teams were brought in, often shown actually 'using' the relevant product. Teams in suits huddled round an Ekco radio looked mildly artificial, but this group dressed up for breakfast and (each with his own packet) seems particularly contrived. Footballers were stars and stars sell products. From these naïve beginnings, product endorsement has come a long way and is now a massive factor in the financial equations of teams and individual players alike.

An oil painting, by Charles Cundall RA, of the 1936 Cup Final in progress. This affords no real detail of the game, even at 25' by 36', but it does very much capture the vibrant feel of a full house at Wembley on Cup Final day in a way a photograph cannot do.

A menu and an invitation for a dinner and dance at the Café Royal 'to celebrate the Final Tie, whatever the result'. Arsenal defeated Division Two Sheffield United with the only goal of the game, scored by Ted Drake. Well over 400 guests, including many of the most senior people in football, sat down to a sumptuous banquet. There was Louis Roederer champagne on offer, in a year in which there was even a full-page advertisement in the programme for champagne. These visits to the Café Royal became regular for Arsenal during their great run of success in the 1930s.

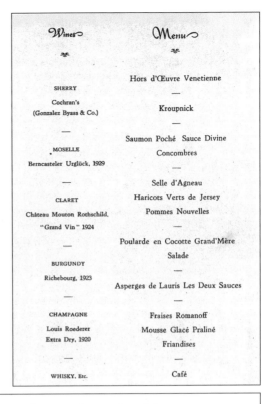

Wines	Menu
	Hors d'Œuvre Venetienne
SHERRY	
Cochran's	Kroupnick
(Gonzalez Byass & Co.)	
	Saumon Poché Sauce Divine
MOSELLE	Concombres
Berncasteler Urglück, 1929	
	Selle d'Agneau
CLARET	Haricots Verts de Jersey
Château Mouton Rothschild,	Pommes Nouvelles
"Grand Vin" 1924	
	Poularde en Cocotte Grand'Mère
BURGUNDY	Salade
Richebourg, 1923	
	Asperges de Lauris Les Deux Sauces
CHAMPAGNE	Fraises Romanoff
Louis Roederer	Mousse Glacé Praliné
Extra Dry, 1920	Friandises
WHISKY, Etc.	Café

To celebrate the FINAL TIE, whatever the result, of the
F.A. CHALLENGE CUP COMPETITION, 1936.

The Directors of Arsenal Football Club

request the honour of the company of

A.J. BOUDEN ESQ

at a DINNER and DANCE at the Café Royal,
Regent Street, London, W.

on Saturday the 25th April, 1936 at 7 for 7.30 p.m.

Morning Dress.   *Please reply by an early post to* The Hon. Secretary,
Dinner Committee,

N.B.—This card will not admit.   28, Sackville Street, W. 1.

A voucher for admission will be sent on receipt of acceptance.

FRIDAY, April 30th.

DEPART—Sunderland - - 11-45 a.m.
Newcastle - - 12-20 p.m.

ARRIVE —King's Cross - - 5-15 p.m.
LUNCH on Train.

MOTOR COACHES will convey Party from King's Cross to Russell Hotel.

No arrangements made for Entertainment after arrival at Russell Hotel.

ıllıllıllıllı
OO

SATURDAY, May 1st.

MOTOR COACHES will leave Russell Hotel at 12 noon for Wembley, and return to Russell Hotel at finish of game.

LUNCH at Wembley Stadium at 1-30 p.m.

SUNDAY, May 2nd.

No arrangements made for Entertainment.

ıllıllıllıllı
OO

MONDAY, May 3rd.

MOTOR COACHES will leave Russell Hotel at 9-15 a.m. for King's Cross.

DEPART—King's Cross - - 9-50 a.m.

ARRIVE —Newcastle - - 2-40 p.m.
Sunderland - - 3-10 p.m.

MOTOR COACHES will convey Party to Roker Park.

Details from the itinerary of the official party for Sunderland's visit to London for the 1937 Final. Despite an excellent record in the League – unbroken membership of Division One and six Championships (including that of 1936) – they had only been in one previous Cup Final. That was in 1913 when they were denied the 'double' by the last team to have done it. There is a stark simplicity about these arrangements with a conspicuous lack of any entertainment.

(Available at Stadium Office Entrance only).
(See Plan on back).

Empire Stadium, Wembley

No. 25

The Football Association Cup Competition

Final Tie

SATURDAY, MAY 1st, 1937

PASS TO DRESSING ROOM

A. J. Elvin

MANAGING DIRECTOR,
Wembley Stadium Limited.

THIS PORTION TO BE RETAINED.

A player's pass to the Wembley dressing rooms for Cup Final day in 1937. It is similar in design to a match ticket but very simply printed in black on white, lacking even the simplest sophistication of security markings. Had it ever occurred to anyone it could very easily have been forged. This particular example was issued to the Sunderland player Len Duns.

The front page of the song sheet from the 1937 Cup Final. After a decade the community singing was now a well-established tradition and Mr J.P. Ratcliff was becoming something of an institution himself. A significant feature of this song sheet is the song in honour of the new king. The loyal address in the Jubilee programme had been followed by the King's death. The new king, Edward VIII, appeared in the 1936 programme, unnamed and with no other comment apart from his patronage of the FA. By 1937 the abdication crisis was over, the new King about to be crowned and a feeling of optimistic relief prevailed. The radio commentator George Allison noted that the whole crowd fell silent to listen to a new tune, *Vivat George the King*, which had been specially composed for the coronation. The composer had given all rights to the National Employment Trust.

An action shot from the 1937 final, showing the Preston goal under pressure.

EASY
TERMS
from
1'-
PER WEEK

STELDENI

PRESTON
N.E. GOALKEEPER'S
FINAL CHOICE

TUTOR

The Preston goalkeeper is pictured here in an advertisement for the Seldini accordion, which appeared in the Cup Final supplement of the *Daily Express*.

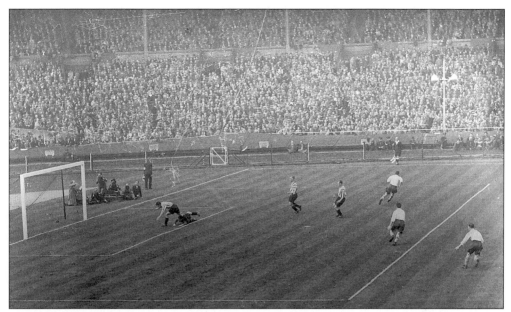

The opening goal scored for Preston by O'Donnell. In a scrappy first half Sunderland had never really seized the initiative and could have been two goals down. Sunderland skipper Carter said afterwards that going a goal down was what finally motivated his team to come back and win. He is reported as saying, 'If you look at our Cup record you will see that we have been a goal down at one time in most of them'.

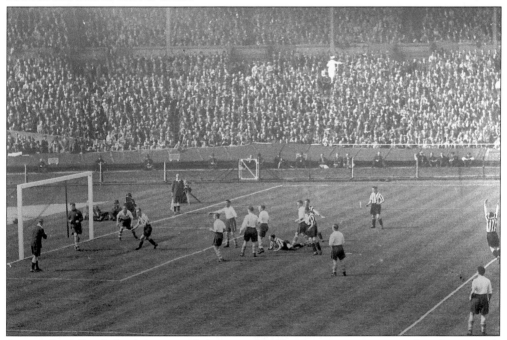

A revitalised Sunderland dominated the second half and, some six minutes after the interval, Bobby Gurney headed home an equaliser after a corner had been headed on to him by Gallacher. A minute later the Sunderland centre forward missed an easy chance to give his side the lead but by this time the momentum was firmly with his men.

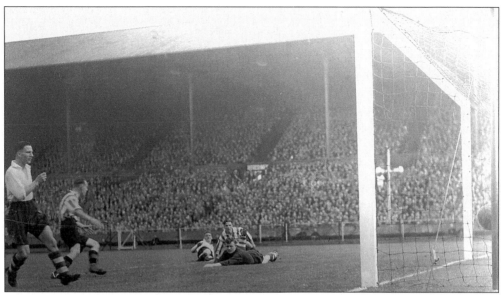

Twenty minutes after Gurney had equalised he coolly supplied a telling pass to enable Raich Carter to score and give Sunderland the lead. Beaten Preston 'keeper Burns can only look on helplessly as the ball reaches the back of the net.

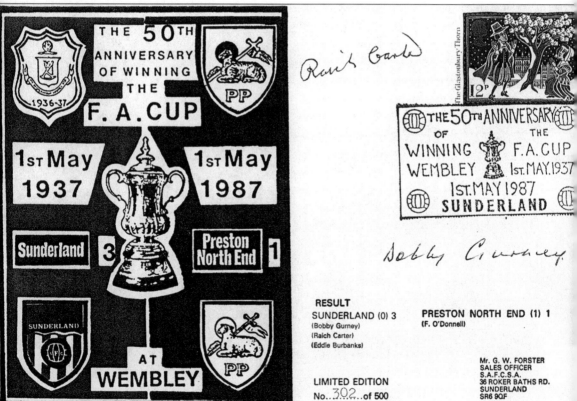

To mark the fiftieth anniversary of the first Cup Final victory a commemorative first day cover was produced. This one has been signed by Carter and Gurney.

With little more than ten minutes to go, and despite a brave fight back by Preston, Sunderland put the game out of reach when Burbanks got the ball from a free-kick and scored Sunderland's third. Note that neither team has numbered jerseys – the fashion which began in 1933 took a while to catch on.

When presenting the Cup to Sunderland captain Carter, Her Majesty said 'That is a nice wedding present for you'!

The classic picture of Sunderland players, triumphant after their first Cup Final victory. Jimmy Gorman is flanked by trainers Dunlop and Reid while fresh-faced Len Duns and elated Sandy McNab carry off their captain and the hitherto elusive trophy. This had been quite a time for Carter. He had played for England at Hampden before the biggest crowd ever assembled for a game in Britain. He had been married the previous Monday and now he had the FA Cup. When presenting it the new Queen said, 'That is a nice wedding present for you.'

Jubilant Sunderland fans leaving Wembley.

The menu card from the lunch at Wembley prior to the 1937 Cup Final. The food itself was very simple, especially when compared with some of the lavish exotica from post-final indulgences. Of more interest is the range of beverages on offer and the prices charged for them. These may seem absurdly cheap by today's standards, but weren't so in 1937.

WINE LIST

CHAMPAGNES.					Bot.	½ Bot.
IRROY, Carte d'Or			1923		22/6	12/-
GEORGE GOULET, Ex. Quality, Ex. Dry			1923		22/6	12/-
Graves, Monosec, Dry	...	...		...	5/-	3/-
St. Julien	...	...	...	...	6/-	3/6
Beaune, Superior	...	...	1919		6/-	3/6
Liqueur Brandy, V.O.	...	...	...	...		2/-
Cognac Brandy, Courvoisier's	...	...	...			1/3
Whisky, Proprietary Brands	...	...	...			9d.
Gin	...	...	...	...		9d.
Port, Croft's No. 1	...	...	...	...		1/-
Sherry, Gonzalez	...	...	...	...		1/-
Kummel	...	...	...	...		1/6
Benedictine	...	...	...	...		1/6
Creme de Menthe	...	...	...	...		1/6
Bass or Guinness	...	...	...	...		9d.
Lager	...	...	...	...		9d.
Minerals	...	...	...	...		6d.
Apollinaris	...	...	...	...		8d.
do. Baby	...	...	...	...		4d.
Cigars	...	...	...	...	From	1/-
Cigarettes	...	...	...	...	„	1/-

The Empire Stadium
Wembley

MENU

The English Cup—Final Tie

Saturday, 1st May
1937

The jersey worn by Len Duns in the 1937 final. By this time a majority of teams wore special jerseys with club badges on them for their Cup Final appearances. Some players kept the whole jersey as a memento of their big day, whilst others simply kept the badge and used the jersey in future games. It seems that Len Duns was the only player in the Sunderland team that day who managed to hang on to his jersey and badge as the Sunderland council, who had provided the badges, asked for them back afterwards!

Huddersfield Town returned to Wembley in 1938 for their fifth Cup Final. Here, the players and manager pose in an advertisement promoting a leading brand of pen.

A finger-tip save by Holdcroft, the Preston 'keeper, from Huddersfield Town winger Beasley.

An action shot from the 1938 Final between Preston and Huddersfield. Preston had knocked out the mighty Arsenal at Highbury en route to a second successive Cup Final appearance and Huddersfield, at the same ground, had knocked out the previous winners Sunderland in the semi-final. This was to be a game with a dramatic climax and, remarkably, reversed the result when the teams had met previously in 1922 – the first final to be decided by a penalty. That penalty had been in the 67th minute. In 1938 it was in the last minute of extra-time.

An action shot from the 1938 final, showing the tenacious Preston right half Shankly (who was to go on and achieve such remarkable success as a manager with Liverpool). Like another giant of post-war management, Shankly played in two successive pre-war finals, first as loser then as winner: Busby had done so for Manchester City in 1933 and 1934. In management, Shankly will always be associated with Liverpool, but he cut his managerial teeth elsewhere – including Huddersfield.

Player portraits from the superb menu card produced for the dinner on Saturday 30 April 1938 in honour of Huddersfield's appearance in the Cup Final. This took place at the Hotel Grand Central and, despite the defeat, seems to have been a splendid occasion in the presence of distinguished guests. Town's outside right Joe Hulme had played in his fifth final, the previous four being for Arsenal. Jerome and his band provided the music and entertainment included 'The Barera Trio, Thrills on Wheels'.

Hulme had packed five Cup finals into just eleven years but his new manager Clem Stephenson was involved in his sixth final. Stephenson, more perhaps than anyone, straddles the whole period, having played in the first final after the First World War and taken his team, as manager, to the penultimate final before the Second World War. Signed from Blyth Spartans as a twenty-year-old in 1910, he played in his first Cup final for Aston Villa in 1913, at the height of the Crystal Palace era. He got two more winners medals in the Stamford Bridge finals, firstly against, and then two years later for Huddersfield. In 1928 came a runners-up medal after which he became manager at Leeds Road from 1929 until 1942, during which time he took his side to two further finals.

A homemade Preston North End rosette from the 1938 Cup Final. While there is ample pictorial evidence that the fans who visited the metropolis for Cup Finals wore rosettes, funny hats and even bow ties (see page 69), there was no tradition of banners, flags, or the larger paraphernalia so much in evidence at modern finals. Perhaps the one thing that would be waved by the crowds at appropriate moments was their free song sheet. This rosette is no crepe paper or even cloth affair, but a hand-knitted woollen one. The letters PNE are knitted into the basic design.

The badge taken from the jersey worn in the 1938 Final by Jack Barclay, the Huddersfield Town inside left. It depicts a magnificent heraldic arms with a Latin motto beneath 'Iuvat Impigros Deus'. Sadly, this has long since been replaced by a much-simplified badge with the name of the club instead of the Latin. With the club's rise through the divisions and move to a splendid, if small, new ground maybe the force of the Latin words is coming into play again!

A signed portrait of Bert Barlow, who played in the 1939 Cup Final. Note that he appears here wearing a Wolverhampton strip. He was transferred to Portsmouth during the last full pre-war season and ended up in the final helping to defeat his former club, for whom he had only made three first-team appearances. Barlow enjoyed further success with Pompey after the war and, later still, played for Colchester when they first entered the Football League.

EMPIRE STADIUM
WEMBLEY

FINAL TIE

OF THE FOOTBALL
ASSOCIATION CHALLENGE
CUP COMPETITION

SATURDAY,
APRIL 29th,
1939

PORTSMOUTH
v.
WOLVERHAMPTON WANDERERS

OFFICIAL PROGRAMME SIXPENCE

The programme cover from the 1939 Final. Fleetway Press had retained the contract for the programmes in the years leading up to the war, but their covers had often been dull and uninspired, especially those of 1936 and 1937. For 1938 and 1939, Baxter's drawings of players lent some human interest to the covers. Two versions of the latter exist, though the difference is much less obvious than in 1933 (see page 102). On the majority of covers, the drawn players and much of the text is in navy blue ink, but on some it is black.

The Wolves team for the 1939 Cup Final. Managed by the redoubtable Major Frank Buckley and containing some stars, such as Stan Cullis (who would himself become such a powerful manager), the Wolves were hot favourites to win. They were runners-up in the League whereas Portsmouth had struggled. On their way to Wembley Wolves had brushed aside lowly Leicester 5-1, Liverpool 4-1 and even League Champions Everton 3-0.

The unfancied Portsmouth side that sought an FA Cup final victory at the third attempt in 1939. Only Worrall remained from their team which had lost five years earlier to Manchester City. Underdogs as they were, this team had only conceded a single goal on their way to the final and that was in the semi-final against the previous year's finalists Huddersfield.

An advertisement from the 1939 Cup Final programme, which shows how far things had moved on with the coverage of finals. Sound could now be assumed and the newsreel companies now worked together to maximise effective distribution with names from the early days, such as Topical Budget, now vanished. Unlike for some of the early finals, where footage once known to have existed is now lost, that from most of the 1930s finals has survived. It would still be many years before television coverage became an option for any significant number of people.

An action shot of Anderson scoring Portsmouth's second goal, just before half-time, past Scott, the League's tallest 'keeper. Former Wolves player Barlow, who was inspired and inspiring against his old club, had opened the scoring after half an hour and within a minute of the resumption he put Scott under such pressure that Parker, following up, put the game beyond doubt.

King George presents the FA Cup to Portsmouth captain Jimmy Guthrie. Next to the King is the secretary of the FA, who had refereed the final five years earlier (which was, of course, Portsmouth's previous Wembley appearance, against Manchester City).

Crowds of delighted supporters welcome back manager Jack Tinn, captain Jimmy Guthrie and the victorious Portsmouth team to Guildhall Square after their emphatic 4-1 win over Wolves in 1939. Portsmouth had at last got their hands on the FA Cup, but events were unfolding which would mean that no one had a chance to take it from them for seven more years. In the July of 1939, skipper Guthrie was involved in a serious motor accident having defied a ban on players using cars during blackout practice. He recovered in time to watch the start of what would prove to be a very short following season.

NATIONAL SERVICE

A Message to All

THE world is in a very disturbed state and nobody can be sure what will happen. One thing is certain, this state of affairs means possible danger of war. If this should happen you should understand that the danger and horror of modern warfare may be brought to your own door.

These dangers can be met and defeated if everybody knows right away what to do and how to do it. There is only one way to find out. Put your name down at once for some form of National Service and get yourself trained in the job you can do best. It is an appeal to your own common-sense to protect your home and your family. It is your duty to do so. It is absolutely necessary for your future.

There are serious deficiencies in the ranks of the Defence Services. In particular, the Air Raid Precaution Services need more Wardens, Stretcher Bearers, Rescue Workers, Decontamination Squads, and Auxiliary Firemen. The Territorial Army needs additional volunteers to bring its strength up to the standard recently agreed upon. Do not think that because your occupation is included in the Schedule of Reserved Occupations that you are debarred from enrolling for National Service. Everyone can undertake some form of National Service. If you are in doubt you can obtain advice from the nearest National Service Office.

It is imperative that you should volunteer at once if you have not already done so. Please, therefore, complete an enrolment form as soon as possible. You can obtain one from any Post Office or National Service Office.

This urgent appeal is made to you in the full knowledge that it will not go unheeded.

Page 19 of the 1939 FA Cup final programme. Among all the usual advertisements for Seagers gin, Brylcreem, radios and even televisions, this page captures the contemporary undercurrent of anxiety. The period began dominated by the ethos of victory and the rich and powerful diversity of the Empire. Here it draws to a close with the stark probability that 'the danger and horror of modern warfare might be brought to your own door'. How true that would prove for a great many people before the FA Cup would once again be raised in triumph by a victorious captain at Wembley.